Contest

Over Japan

by Herbert Feis

The Norton Library

W · W · Norton & Company · Inc ·
New York

Published simultaneously in Canada by
George J. McLeod Limited, Toronto

BOOKS THAT LIVE

The Norton imprint on a book means that in the publisher's
estimation it is a book not for a single season but for the years.

W. W. NORTON & COMPANY, INC.

Printed in the United States of America

1 2 3 4 5 6 7 8 9 0

Contents

Foreword   *1*

I. The Circlet of History   *3*

II. Some Primary Texts and Origins   *10*

III. First American Actions and Proposals   *22*

IV. Stalemate at London   *31*

V. Interim Responses   *51*

VI. Harriman Talks with Stalin   *59*

VII. The Wearisome Interim Negotiations   *67*

VIII. If At First You Don't Succeed—   *78*

IX. Moscow—The Correlated Negotiations   *85*

X. Moscow—The Correlated Negotiations *Continued*   *93*

XI. Moscow—The Accord About Japan   *107*

XII. The Reception of the Moscow Accord   *111*

XIII. Truman Takes Offense   *119*

XIV. The Contest Carried On   *127*

Appendices   *153*

Foreword

Many persons in and out of government assisted me in the effort to tell of this contest over Japan between the United States and the Soviet Union at the outset of the Cold War. Of these I wish particularly to thank Ambassador W. Averell Harriman, former Secretary of State James F. Byrnes, and former Ambassador William J. Sebald for their generous help. Mrs. Virginia M. Rowe sustained with her customary good nature and reliability the secretarial and typing work. My wife Ruth S-B. Feis has helped in many ways, especially by her cheerful assurance that any book of mine is well worth the effort and should be read.

The preliminary research for this book was done at the same time as that for my previous book, *The Atomic Bomb and the End of World War II*. But I delayed publishing in the hope that postponement would bring forth important additional source material—a hope that has not yet been realized.

Herbert Feis

York, Maine

I

The Circlet of History

This is a narrative about the contest between the United States and the Soviet Union after World War II for the right to direct the policies of Japan during the period of occupation (1945–1952).

Before starting, let us round quickly the circlet of history within which Japan has abided with the United States and Russia. Let us recall its main features and thereby be reminded—as a lesson in perspective—how inconstant the relations between these states have been. The student may not be able to resist the impression that—as in other tales of the contortions of nations—history resembles the earnest reminiscences of a troupe of tumblers.

During the war between Japan and Czarist Russia in 1904–1905, most Americans wanted the Japanese to win. They remembered ties of trade that went back half a century, to the time when well-meaning American intruders led by Commodore Perry and his black ships had hauled Japan toward the Western world. They admired the pluck and disciplined diligence of the Japanese people. They appreciated why the Japanese on their four small and poor islands should feel compelled to seek advantages on the adjoining mainland of

Asia. Painters and writers were charmed by the grace of their demeanor, their dress, their architecture and ways of life.

In contrast, most Americans thought of Russia as a crude and oppressive imperialist nation, a vast land with tremendous but poorly utilized resources, inhabited by a vigorous people from whom there came men and women of the greatest gifts, who were withal boorish and superstitious. Russia had absorbed many races and tribes and pushed its borders far into Europe and far into Asia; and yet its dynasty continued to seek to sprawl further. These were the prevailing notions and sentiments that had approved Theodore Roosevelt's initiative to end the war between Russia and Japan while Japan was still winning and could secure a settlement helpful to its prospects and position.

True, Japan had made war on China and acquired Formosa (Taiwan) as prize. It had invaded Korea and brought its people under domination. But at that time Japan appeared to have no further designs upon China—perhaps only because it lacked the power and the resources. In contrast, Russia had contended with the Western imperialists to secure control over adjacent regions of China—particularly the vast provinces of Manchuria. The preservation of Chinese independence and integrity was one of the prime and determined ends of American diplomacy.

Thus, in the first decade of the century, the American Government had favored Japan as against Russia. A few publicists and prophets of the "yellow peril" aroused uneasiness about Japanese intentions. But almost all Americans continued to hold Japan in friendly admiration until the Japanese covertly tried during World War I to extend their control over a crumpled China. Even thereafter, American fears and suspicions were temporarily allayed, when in 1922 Japan joined in the Washington Treaties. These were conceived to be a dependable basis for order in the Pacific. Japanese statesmanship, it was hopefully thought, had entered into another era of peaceful ways and comity with the West.

4

During the next decade the friction between Russia and Japan revived, as they quarreled over the respective realms of possession or influence in land areas adjoining Russia, particularly Manchuria and Mongolia.

The period of relaxation in tension between the United States and Japan did not last long. They began to watch mistrustfully each other's power positions in the Central Pacific, and in the waters near the Philippines and the outposts that the United States had acquired from Spain. But American policy continued to be cautiously friendly, until in the nineteen-thirties the Japanese fell under the thrall of military leaders and dreams of dominating all of Asia. American good will ebbed as the Japanese invasion of China expanded in an effort to compel the Chinese to be obedient to Japanese wishes. It drained off entirely when Japan joined its forces with those of Hitler's Germany and Mussolini's Italy, and thus became a partner in the brutish effort to break down Britain and France and their empires. When in 1941 Japan would not renounce its ambitions or alliances, and instead struck the American installations at Pearl Harbor and the Philippines, war tragically came. These links in the circlet of history which had once glowed with charm now blazed with fire.

Resistance to the Axis brought the United States and the Soviet Union together during World War II. When, after Pearl Harbor, the Soviet Government said it would not at once join in the war on Japan, the American Government was disappointed. But it accepted the decision because of the wish to have the Soviet Union hold out against the Nazi assault from the west. Ideologies and animosities were temporarily ignored. The United States provided the Soviet Union with materials and supplies needed to sustain the civilian population and war production, and with combat equipment for which American and Allied forces themselves had urgent need. By 1943–1944, the Soviet Union, confident that it had repelled the German assault, promised that it would enter the war against Japan. Thereupon the American Government agreed to send great shipments of oil and military supplies for the Soviet armies that were to be assembled in Manchuria.

In Europe as the end of the war came clearly into sight, Russian military movements were influenced by the wish to achieve territorial and political aims by military possession. Britain's Prime Minister Winston Churchill in the last months of the war pleaded with the American authorities to use Allied forces opposingly. But they refused to risk a confrontation that might hurt the prospect of preserving postwar collaboration.

But in the Far East it was only in the last months of the war (particularly in the fortnight after the test in July of the atomic bomb) that military decisions or plans of either the United States or the Soviet Union were deflected by forethought about postwar political settlements in regard to Japan or adjacent realms of the Asian mainland. Up to then Moscow had been pleased by American military successes and advances in the Pacific; Washington had been pleased by developments that brought clear anticipation of Russian entry into the Pacific war.

Even when final victory over Japan seemed assured and near, the Soviet Union and the United States had not dealt with one another as rival claimants or antagonists for the right to occupy or control Japan after the war. The Russians, the American Government had assumed, would be satisfied by the transfer of those parts of the Japanese Empire promised it by the agreement which President Franklin Delano Roosevelt had made with Premier Joseph Stalin at Yalta in February, 1945.

By the time (after July 16) the American authorities were sure that they possessed a new weapon of incomparably greater power than any known before, and would not need Soviet cooperation for quick victory, the arrangements for Soviet participation in the Pacific war were too far along to cancel. Moreover, the men who directed American military affairs believed that the Russians would enter the war whether or not bidden to do so. Better, then, to have them enter as soon as they would, and thereby save American lives. The senior officials of the American Army in particular continued to be apprehensive over the casualties that would be incurred in an invasion of the Japanese home islands, and in the residual task of subduing the Japanese armies on the Asian mainland. They did not foresee that the war would be brought to so abrupt an end by the atomic bomb, and that at a single command by the Emperor, Japanese combat forces everywhere would surrender and give up their arms.

Thus, up to the very day of Soviet entry into the war, up to the moment of Japanese acceptance of unconditional surrender, the American Government continued to facilitate Soviet participation in the war against Japan. The spheres of operation of American and Soviet naval and air forces agreed on by their Chiefs of Staff at Potsdam late in July seem to have been determined by military circumstances and calculations.

Both the American and Soviet Governments knew that the final direct assault on the Japanese home islands was to be made by the forces of the United States and its Western allies. Still, there had been no discussion or accord about their respective right to direct and control Japan during the period of occupation which was to follow victory.

However, Truman, impressed by what he had learned at Potsdam about the range of Soviet claims and Stalin's stubborn and determined insistence upon them, formed a definite resolution. This was that there should not be in Japan any joint system of control such as had been set up in Germany; that even if our allies provided contingents for the occupation forces they would have to be under a unified American command; and that there were to be no separate zones of occupation in Japan.

7

Truman —
after Potsdam

In words he used in his *Memoirs*, he was "determined that the Japanese occupation should not follow in the footsteps of our German experience." [1]

The American officers in command of the operation in Guam and Tinian had been authorized to use the atomic bomb at any time "after about" August 1. But bad weather had delayed its use. It was dropped on Hiroshima on August 6, and on Nagasaki on August 9 (Tokyo time).

Stalin was still bargaining with T. V. Soong, the Chinese Prime Minister, over the precise nature and range of Soviet rights and concessions in Manchuria. He was trying to confirm not merely the rewards which at Yalta Roosevelt had promised, but a dilated interpretation of them. But as soon as the great power of the bomb was demonstrated, the Soviet Government hurried to be in at the kill. Giving specious reasons, V. M. Molotov, the Commissar for Foreign Affairs, with wooden face and abrupt manner on the afternoon of August 8, gave the Japanese Ambassador in Moscow a statement which ended with the affirmation that "In view of the foregoing, the Soviet government declares that as of tomorrow, that is of 9 August, the Soviet Union will consider it is in a state of war with Japan." In fact, Stalin did not wait for the message to be received in Tokyo; the first Soviet troops had crossed the frontiers of Manchuria from east and west.

There can be little doubt that the Soviet Government had previously reckoned that the war would continue long enough to enable the powerful Soviet armies to drive the Japanese out of Manchuria and force those in Korea to surrender to them. Then the Soviet Union would have been in a position not only to have China accede to its wishes, but also to support a claim for an important part in the occupation and control of Japan.

The preponderance of evidence that it was the shock of the atomic bombs that caused Japan to capitulate while its

[1] Harry S Truman, *Year of Decisions*, Vol. I of *Memoirs*, Garden City, New York, Doubleday & Company, 1955, p. 432.

armies were in the field has not deterred Soviet authorities from trying to perpetuate the legend that it was the Soviet march into Manchuria which really caused the Japanese to surrender.[2]

The explosion of the atomic bombs did not completely arrest Russian military movements. But it left the Soviet authorities with a pretension to share in the occupation of Japan rather than a valid right—valid in the traditional sense that where a nation has given lives of its people, for no matter what cause, it is entitled, after victory, to rule.

In other ways the abrupt end of the war was to turn out disadvantageously for the United States. Had it gone on longer, American forces might well have been in a position to land more quickly in Korea and occupy more of that country. And it is probable that, nurtured by us, the armies of the Chinese National Government would have been stronger, better equipped, and better organized to occupy more of their country. They might have been able to bring the Chinese Communists into an acceptable coalition arrangement. But these are roving conjectures. The situation as it actually was, not as it might have been, determined what happened at the very beginning of the contest between the American and Soviet Governments over the exercise of control of Japan. This contest began as soon as Japan admitted defeat.

[2] Of the many repetitions of this standard myth, the latest that comes to my attention is a statement in an article by Soviet Defense Minister Marshal Rodion Malinovsky in *Izvestia:* "Imperialist Japan was compelled to capitulate not because of the U. S. atomic blows on Hiroshima and Nagasaki, which senselessly exterminated hundreds of thousands of persons, but as a result of the decisive blows on the land front in Manchuria." (Boston *Globe*, June 23, 1966.)

II

Some Primary Texts and Origins

The discussions between the American Government and its allies about the control of Japan during the occupation often reverted to precedent declarations, accords, and orders. These, it was understood, would govern the policies to be pursued and the nature of their association in the exercise of control.

Of the oft-cited texts, we need remind ourselves only of the most important, and at this point only sparingly.[1]

Two had a connective rather than a direct bearing on the contest for control. One was the Cairo Declaration of December, 1943, signed by Roosevelt, Churchill, and Chiang Kai-shek. This had expressed the resolve of the three Allies to

[1] In this narrative I shall cite the texts of these agreements only to the minimum extent necessary to explain essential issues. Similarly, when describing the arguments which used texts as briefs I shall condense the substance of these texts. The documents which are relevant and in some measure basic are at least fifteen. The texts of most but not all of them are conveniently assembled in Appendix A of the Report of the Government Section of Supreme Commander for the Allied Powers entitled *Political Reorientation of Japan*, Washington, D. C., 1948.

For ready reference the texts of those few orders, agreements, and proposals about which the contest traced in this narrative focused, are included as appendices in this book.

bring unrelenting pressure upon Japan until they obtained "unconditional surrender." It stipulated that ". . . Japan shall be stripped of all the islands in the Pacific which she has seized or occupied since the beginning of the first World War in 1914, and that all the territories Japan has stolen from the Chinese, such as Manchuria, Formosa, and the Pescadores, shall be restored to the Republic of China. Japan will also be expelled from all other territories which she has taken by violence and greed."[2] This was to be the doom of the Japanese Empire. Shortly after acceding to this Declaration, Stalin had secretly reassured Roosevelt and Churchill that he intended to join them in the Pacific war as soon as Germany was defeated, so that "then we shall be able by our common front to defeat Japan."

The other was the secret agreement reached (at Yalta in February, 1945) between Roosevelt and Stalin and signed by Churchill with demur.[3] This enumerated the Japanese territories in the Far East to be turned over to the Soviet Union (the southern part of Sakhalin and the Kurile Islands), and defined the special rights to be accorded in Manchuria, and the future status of Outer Mongolia. These were the premiums to be paid Russia for entering the Pacific war and for expressing its readiness to conclude a pact of friendship and alliance with the National Government of China.

Other texts were explicitly concerned with the future of Japan. The most basic was the Potsdam Declaration, issued in July, 1945. While calling in most ominous tones on the Japanese to surrender, it informed them in general terms of the treatment they should expect after surrender and of the nature of the intended occupation. The text of this Declaration had been composed by the American authorities after many months of deliberation. But, when issued with the ready concurrence of Churchill and Chiang Kai-shek, it spoke for

[2] Text in Appendix 1.
[3] Text in Appendix 2.

them as well as for Truman.[4]

Another was the general statement of surrender, supplementing and interpreting the Potsdam Declaration, which the Japanese Government accepted on August 14.[5] This also had been composed by the American Government. After the most important of the amendments which it proposed had been accepted, the British Government approved it. And, as we shall see, after the rebuff of the attempt by Stalin and Molotov to temporize and change one vital point, the Soviet Government had also acquiesced and asked to be included among its sponsors.

Another was the General Order No. 1 issued on September 2 by the Japanese Emperor under orders from the Supreme Commander, General Douglas MacArthur.[6] This was a comprehensive plan designating the particular Allied authority to whom the Japanese forces in each area were to surrender. It was communicated to the British, Chinese, and Soviet Governments, at whose behest minor changes were made.

Still another was the United States Initial Post-Surrender Policy for Japan (sent to MacArthur at the end of August).[7] This instruction by the American Government set out the connections which were to prevail between the American and Allied Governments in the direction of the occupation, in concert. As will be shown, when the British and Soviet Governments grasped its aims, they protestingly made known that they were not pleased with their subordination, and proposed other arrangements. The ensuing contest of ideas and desires went on until almost the end of the occupation; it is that contest which we are setting out to describe.

These agreements and texts left a large area in which the diplomatic tussle could and did take place. While they did

[4] Text in Appendix 3.
[5] Text in Appendix 4.
[6] Text in Appendix 5.
[7] Text in Appendix 6.

roughly set the limits and define the main form and purposes of the authority to be exercised over occupied Japan, they were not precise. Other governments—especially the Soviet Government—did not feel obligated to accept the American interpretation of many points. Thus their implementation (that awful but useful word) was affected by the political and military quivers of the nations and by the impact of accident.

The resolution of the Americans to have decisive say in the control of Japan was first openly and firmly stated in the Potsdam Declaration issued on July 26—the final summons for surrender.

There had been previously some slight worry lest the Soviet Government try to diminish either our victory or our chance to determine what was to be done about Japan after victory. One of the purposes which had led President Truman to send Harry Hopkins to Moscow at the end of May, 1945, was to ascertain whether the Soviet Government firmly intended to enter the Pacific war. After so saying, Stalin had remarked that since some elements in Japan were putting out peace feelers, he thought the time had come to "consider together our joint attitude and act in concert about the surrender of Japan." [8] He feared, he had added, that Japan would try to divide the Allies. The American Government may at the time have wondered whether this was a hint that the Soviet Government might make a deal with Japan if its wishes were not gratified. Stalin's further comments had indicated a preference for treating Japan harshly and for eliminating all Imperial institutions. He had also revealed that he expected Russia to share in the actual occupation of Japan. He told Hopkins that he thought the American and Soviet Governments would have to have "serious talks about Far Eastern problems, particularly in regard to Japan, including such questions *as the zones of*

[8] Robert E. Sherwood, *Roosevelt and Hopkins, An Intimate History*, New York, Harper and Brothers, 1948, p. 903.

operations for the armies and zones of occupation in Japan." [9] (The italics in the text are mine.) Hopkins had not responded to this comment, and the American Government had ignored it.

The State and War Departments had been long engaged in the preparation of an exposition both of policies that were to be pursued after surrender and of plans for the occupation. Secretary of State James F. Byrnes had taken a text to Potsdam which was little different from that of the ultimatum that was issued. The only significant change—and that a regrettable one—was the erasure of the sentence that indicated that the Japanese might be allowed to retain the Emperor.

The Potsdam Declaration was a conjoined ultimatum and a general exposition of the way in which Japan and the Japanese would be treated after surrender. The President had told Stalin a day or two before it was issued that such a declaration was going to be addressed to the Japanese. But he had not consulted him about its contents or phraseology, nor asked him to subscribe to it. When Molotov complained because Byrnes released it without obtaining Soviet concurrence, the Secretary of State blandly explained that he had done so because the Soviet Government was not yet at war with Japan, and he did not wish to embarrass it. This fact might have been conclusive of itself. But Truman and his advisers were by then all determined that the Russians should not be given the chance to delay or impede the surrender. Moreover, the President, upset by Stalin's inordinate claims—the stretch of his will to dominate—did not want to associate the Soviet Government any more closely than need be with the future exercise of control over Japan. By then the atomic bomb had been tested, and while the Americans still thought Soviet entry

[9] *Papers Relating to the Foreign Relations of the United States: Conference of Berlin (Potsdam)*, 2 vols., Washington, D. C., 1960. Document 26, Bohlen memo of Stalin-Hopkins talk, May 28, 1945.

into the war would be useful, they no longer felt it essential to victory or the preservation of many American lives.

Had Stalin's concurrence in the Declaration been sought before issuance, it is likely that he would have proposed some changes, and unlikely that they could have been agreed upon in a hurry. Right then and there the contention over the control of Japan might well have come into the open.

Probably Stalin would have excused himself from subscribing to the Declaration unless its issuance was delayed until after the Soviet entry into the Pacific war. His subsequent behavior indicated his determination to have the Soviet armies take an active part in the final days of the Japanese defeat.

But suppose Stalin's concurrence had been obtained? Would he have subscribed publicly to the ultimatum? If so, would subsequent events have gone differently? Who is to know? Had he agreed to do so, the Japanese acceptance of the ultimatum conceivably would have been more immediate; but improbably so, since the Japanese were not assured about the future of the Imperial institution.

The next intimation of American purpose evoked the first definite signs of clashing desire. After the bombs had been dropped on Hiroshima and Nagasaki, the Japanese Government asked the American Government to clarify a few provisions in the demand for unconditional surrender as set forth in the Potsdam Declaration. The reply drafted in urgent haste indicated that the Imperial institutions could be maintained if the Japanese people so desired. On the night of August 10 (while the whole world was intently waiting for the end of the war) before transmitting to Tokyo its proposed answer to the Japanese query, the American Government asked the Soviet Government (which had entered the war only two or three days before)—as well as its other allies—to subscribe to it. One passage read, ". . . the authority of the Emperor and the Japanese Government to rule the state shall be subject to the Supreme Commander of the Allied powers who will take such steps as he deems proper to effectuate the surrender terms."

The American Ambassador to Moscow, W. Averell Harriman, was asked to get an instant answer. Though Stalin had told Hopkins a few months before that he thought the Emperor should be deposed, Molotov did not now renew that contention. But his response raised the issue of how control over Japan was to be exercised. He said, "The Soviet Government also considers that, in case of an affirmative reply from the Japanese Government, the Allied powers *should* [or *"must"*] reach an agreement on the *candidacy* or *candidacies* for representation of the Allied High Command to which the Japanese Emperor and the Japanese Government are to be subordinated." [10] When Harriman asked him what he meant, Molotov explained that it was necessary to reach an agreement as to which Allied representative or representatives would deal with the Japanese. He proposed that the American Government should make a suggestion and that the Allies could subsequently agree as to who the Supreme Commander was to be.

Harriman said this would give the Soviet Government a chance to veto the choice of the Supreme Commander, that this was utterly out of the question, and that he knew the American Government would not agree to it. He asked Molotov whether the Soviet Government would be willing to have MacArthur as Supreme Commander. Molotov said he thought so but he would have to consult his colleagues. Harriman repeated that as the Soviet answer read, it seemed to mean that the Soviet Government was asking for the right to veto the selection, and he was sure this would not be acceptable to the American Government. Molotov then remarked that it was conceivable that there might be two Supreme

[10] The Russian translator (Pavlov) in reading the English version to Harriman used the word "must." But the Russian word may have either meaning, or an indefinite intermediate one.

The italics are mine.

Commanders—General MacArthur and Marshal Vasilevski, commander of Soviet forces in the Far East. Harriman said that was "absolutely inadmissible." Before Harriman could report on this conversation to Washington, he received by telephone a message from Molotov saying that he had talked with Stalin, that the Soviet Government had intended to suggest only that there should be "consultation" before the selection of a Supreme Commander, not a requirement for "reaching an agreement."

The revised text of the Soviet answer sent to Harriman read, "The Soviet Government also considers that, in the case of an affirmative reply from the Japanese Government, the Allied powers should consult on the candidacy for representation of the Allied High Command to which the Japanese Emperor and the Japanese Government are to be subordinated." To this the American Government made no objection. It hurried off its answer to the waiting Japanese rulers. They, in desperate sorrow, thereupon accepted the terms of surrender.

The American Government hastened at once to inform its three great allies that it intended to designate General MacArthur to be the Supreme Commander for the Allied Forces in Japan. All agreed to the selection and appointment.

The American Government also rushed out to MacArthur an instruction in regard to the procedure for carrying the surrender into full and formal effect. This informed him that the governments of China, Great Britain, and the Soviet Union had been asked to send representatives to the place of surrender. Paragraphs 5 and 6 conveyed his supreme authority.

> 5) From the moment of surrender, the authority
> of the Emperor and the Japanese Government to rule
> the state will be subject to you and you will take such

steps as you deem proper to effectuate the surrender terms.

6) You will exercise supreme command over all land, sea and air forces which may be allocated for enforcement in Japan of the surrender terms by the Allied Powers concerned.[11]

Copies of this order were sent to Prime Minister Clement Attlee, Stalin, and Chiang Kai-shek. The Chief of Staff, General George C. Marshall, on informing MacArthur officially of the Japanese capitulation (August 15) notified him that this Directive was in effect at once.

Similarly, on their own initiative and under pressure of circumstances, the Joint Chiefs of Staff sent MacArthur, as Supreme Commander, their first main instruction. This conveyed the text of the order which the Supreme Commander was to require the Japanese Imperial Headquarters to issue, as by the direction of the Emperor. Sent (on the fifteenth) to the other Allied Governments for their comments, it was designated as General Order No. 1. It set down the arrangements to govern the surrender of the widely dispersed Japanese armies. It was a comprehensive plan which designated the Allied authority to whom the Japanese forces in each area were to surrender.

The purpose of this comprehensive plan was to avert confusion and misunderstanding. It lessened the chance that the Japanese commanders might seek to cause dissension among the members of the coalition. It was designed to eliminate possible quarrels between the Allied commanders in the various theaters of war about geographical jurisdiction and penetration of each other's field of command and to prevent competition for shipping and naval support.

This order had been composed without formal discussion

[11] This was entitled *Directive to the Supreme Commander for the Allied Powers for the Occupation of Japan.* It was sent to MacArthur on August 29.

between the American Government and its allies. In deciding the zones of surrender, military circumstances—the location of the land, naval, and air forces of each ally—had been taken into primary account. But its provisions were also deemed to be in conformity with the political agreements that had previously been reached—particularly the Cairo Declaration, the Yalta agreement, and the discussions at Potsdam. And so they were, except for a few minor particulars which had been left in suspense by these prior accords.

Japanese commanders of forces in the Pacific islands south of Japan were to surrender to the Commander-in-Chief of the U. S. Pacific Fleet (Admiral Chester W. Nimitz), and those in command of forces in Japan proper, the southern section of Korea, and the Philippines were to surrender to the Commander-in-Chief, U. S. Army Forces in the Pacific (General MacArthur). In a later complementary order to American commanders, instructing them to proceed to send the occupation forces into Japan, it was stipulated that Marines should be landed on the coast of China to give such help to the Chinese forces to gain control of ports and communications as might be practicable without investment in a major land campaign.

The area allotted to the Soviet Union was spacious enough to reward it for being faithful to the Allies and entering the war after it was amply prepared for the fight. This segment of General Order No. 1 stipulated that the Japanese commanders and all ground, sea, air, and military forces within Manchuria, Korea north of 38 degrees north latitude, Karafuto (southern section of Sakhalin), and most of the Kurile Islands surrender to the Commander-in-Chief of the Soviet Forces in the Far East.

The distribution was on the whole well received by our allies. But each of their governments requested some revision in detail—not only the Soviet Government, but the Chinese, the British, the French, and the Australian.

Stalin, in his reply to Truman (August 16), asked for two "modest" supplements to the Soviet sphere. One was that the

Japanese forces in all—not merely almost all—the Kurile Islands, which were to pass to the possession of the Soviet Government, be instructed to surrender to the Soviet Military Commander. To this, after a ruffling exchange about landing rights in the Kuriles for American planes, President Truman acceded. The other was that the Japanese armed forces in the northern half of the island of Hokkaido (the northernmost of the four Japanese main islands) be directed to surrender to the Commander-in-Chief of the Soviet Forces in the Far East instead of to the Commander-in-Chief of the U. S. Army Forces in the Pacific. In that connection, he explained that "this last point is of special importance to Russian public opinion. As is known, in 1919–21 the Japanese occupied the whole of the Soviet Far East. Russian public opinion would be gravely offended if the Russian troops had no occupation area in any part of the territory of Japan proper."

The President and the Chiefs of Staff rejected this request indignantly, since it would have meant divided occupation and control of Japan. Stalin attuned his acknowledgment to make it sound regretful rather than angry.

By this time, it should be noted, Stalin had signed agreements with the Chinese Nationalist Government to support it alone as the unifying authority in China and to withdraw Soviet troops from Manchuria three months after the end of hostilities. In return, the Soviet Union had secured places in the administration of and rights over the railways and main ports of Manchuria (Dairen and Port Arthur). These would enable it, if it chose, either to dominate Manchuria or to compel Nationalist China to be pliant in return for Soviet restraint. The officials of the State Department concerned with Far Eastern affairs inclined to the belief that Stalin's promises to Chiang Kai-shek would be worth little or nothing more than the military strength and political skill with which Chiang could take over the regions of China that had been occupied by the Japanese and carry out the campaign against the Chinese Communists. Weakness, it was suspected, would embolden Moscow secretly to help the Chinese Communists despite promises to abstain from doing so.

However, the American Government hoped to keep these possibilities of the situation in China separate from the management of Japan. Assuming that the essential policies for Japan had been set down and agreed upon, the American Government, during the two-week interval between capitulation and occupation, went ahead unhesitatingly. It instructed the Supreme Commander how to execute these policies. And it proposed an arrangement for consultation between itself and its allies about the maturation of these policies and their effectuation.

III

First American Actions
and Proposals

Much thought had been given to the arrangements for the occupation and control of Japan. A memorandum conceived in long sessions of State-War-Navy Committee and subcommittees had been endorsed by the Joint Chiefs of Staff. President Truman was pleased with it, and on August 18, two weeks before MacArthur set foot in Japan, approved it.

The main elements were firm though not precisely fixed: 1) The American Government recognized an obligation to consult with those of its allies who had fought against Japan, and to act in concert with them in effecting Japanese surrender and disarmament. 2) Although these allies, thus, had the right and responsibility to share in the determination of policies for Japan, the American Government must be in charge of the execution of these policies. 3) While the United States would provide most of the occupation forces, it wanted our allies to contribute contingents. 4) But all national components of the army of occupation should be combined into a unified force under a commander designated by the American Government. 5) The whole of Japan was to be treated and administered as a unity. 6) There would be no division of control or separate zones of occupation, as in Germany.[1]

The task of carrying these connected conceptions into the actual conduct of Japanese affairs was a triangular one. The American Government had to try to please—or at least to placate—not only its allies but also the imperious Supreme Commander in Tokyo. In conformity with this memo there were composed in the fortnight before the official surrender (on September 2) two documents designed to do so.

One, briefly noted among the primary texts, was the instruction to MacArthur which set down the policies he was to make effective during—as it was then conceived—the initial period after surrender. This had been composed after several months of discussions that were far from relaxed.[2] MacArthur had been given ample chance to express his opinions about its many sections and points. He had protested provisions that might hamper him in the exercise of his judgment in the light of uncertain circumstances. With enough reason he found that some were "unwise, rigid, too detailed and unnecessary." General Marshall patiently explained why detailed and comprehensive instructions were deemed necessary. The State Department, he advised MacArthur, was the primary sponsor of some of the troubling points, because it believed it essential to acknowledge the attentive interest of other governments in the course pursued and the actions taken. Moreover, Marshall pointed out that precision was necessary to enable the several civilian government departments of the American Government and the military command to work together smoothly. In a continuous—against a deadline—weekend session, driven along by Assistant Secretary of War John J. McCloy, various sections were simplified and shortened, and the whole made more coherent.

[1] This memorandum was called *National Composition of Forces to Occupy Japan Proper in the Post-War Period*.

[2] *United States Initial Post-Surrender Policy for Japan*. Sent to MacArthur on August 29, 1945, and formally approved by President Truman on September 6. Text in Appendix 6.

There was reason for believing that this instruction would give satisfaction to our allies. Since its text is so well known and has been so fully examined and commented on in the intervening years, it would be wearisome to restate here its many crammed sections. To understand and appraise what happened subsequently, it will suffice to select a few provisions which, it was thought, would appeal strongly to the Soviet Government, and a few which, it turned out, were challenged later by it.

The detachment of the Japanese Empire was confirmed. One provision read, "Japan's sovereignty will be limited to the islands of Honshu, Hokkaido, Kyushu, Shikoku and such minor outlying islands as may be determined, in accord with the Cairo Declaration. . . ." This left the way open for permanent acquisition by the Russians of those parts of the Japanese Empire as had been promised at Yalta—and more.

Another paragraph stipulated that Japan was to be completely disarmed and demilitarized. "Japan is not to have an army, navy, air force, secret police organization, or any civil aviation."

These and other provisions that buttressed them should have dissipated fears and suspicions that Japan, abetted by the United States, might again become a threat to the security of the Soviet Union or peace in the Pacific. But they did not dull the blade of doubt. The Soviet Government did not cease to suspect that this excellent general statement of policies and objectives masked a wish to turn Japan again into an antagonist of the Soviet Union. In this, as in so many other areas, the Soviet Union showed extreme uneasiness about the emergence of any power that might alone, or in combination, challenge it. This had its roots perhaps in the experience of Western and Japanese interference after the Bolshevik revolution and in memories of the Nazi invasion. But by September, 1945, there was no longer any genuine reason for a sense of insecurity. Nor did the Soviet authorities continue, I believe, genuinely to feel threatened. What they really disliked was the dominating presence in Japan of the United States—which might oppose their will and thwart their own pushful designs.

That all our allies would be expected to accept a subordinate role was indicated by several provisions of this instruction to MacArthur. Most explicit was one paragraph in the section named "Allied Authority," which, in conformity with the ideas stated in the source memo, read, "Although every effort will be made, by consultation and by constitution of appropriate advisory bodies, to establish policies for the conduct of the occupation and the control of Japan which will satisfy the principal Allied powers, in the event of any differences of opinion among them, the policies of the United States will govern."

That the American Government was going to try to shape the future of Japanese life and society along lines of Western democracy—liberal or semi-socialist—was evidenced by the whole tenor of the instruction. Individual liberties and democratic political forms and procedures—as understood in the United States—were to be encouraged and maintained. Favor was to be "shown to the development of organizations in labor, industry, and agriculture, organized on a democratic basis. Policies shall be favored which permit a wide distribution of income and of the ownership of the means of production and trade."

These policies obviously debarred a Communist take-over from within Japan, even as the American presence debarred a take-over from without. They set up the only strong barrier to Communist domination of the whole of Northeast Asia. Not only that; should Japan while pursuing these policies recover, thrive, and regain influence in the Far East, resistance to Communism elsewhere in Asia would take note and heed.

This instruction was dispatched to MacArthur a very few days before the formal surrender and his assumption of authority. Because the war had ended so much sooner than had been anticipated, and because the discussions within the American Government had gone on until the very verge of surrender, our allies were not given an advance opportunity to comment upon it. If they had been, the resultant negotiations would have been prolonged, and almost certainly inconclusive. The American Government was unwilling to risk confusion at the last moment, or to risk paralysis of action during the crucial first weeks of occupation.

But it had not been forgetful of its obligation to consult with its allies, and to decide policies by common consent. Having limited in effect the scope of possible derangement of its purposes, the American Government invited full discussion within the perimeter of policy drawn in this primary statement.

The Allied governments [3] had been asked on August 21 to join in the creation of a Far Eastern Advisory Commission.[4] As then conceived by the American Government, this Commission *would make representations to the member governments* about: 1) the formulation of policies, principles, and standards by which the fulfillment by Japan of its obligations under the terms of surrender might be determined. 2) the steps necessary and the machinery required to insure the strict compliance by Japan with the provisions of the instrument of surrender. 3) such other matters as might be assigned to it *by agreement* of the participating governments.

The proposal did not explicitly state what procedure was to be followed after the participating governments had received the recommendations.

Harriman, who had been alerted by Stalin's quick reach for a share in the occupation, surmised that he would argue over the terms of this proposal. Therefore, although he was

[3] The U.S.S.R., China, Great Britain, France, The Netherlands, Canada, Australia, New Zealand, and the Philippines.

[4] A detailed account of the provisions of the original American proposal and of the evolution of its terms of reference and procedure is in Chapter I of Department of State Publication 5138, *The Far Eastern Commission. A Study in International Cooperation: 1945 to 1952*, by Dr. George H. Blakeslee, Far Eastern Series 60, Washington, D. C., 1953.

eager to discuss his personal plans with his superiors in Washington, he informed Byrnes that he believed he should remain in Moscow until agreement had been reached on the control machinery for Japan. He recalled that when he had rebuffed Molotov's suggestion that there might be a joint supreme command consisting of General MacArthur and Marshal Vasilevski, he had said that he was sure that the United States would always be ready to consult with the Soviet authorities, but could not agree to give them a veto. The proposal for a joint command had been quickly dropped, but Harriman was convinced that the Soviet authorities had others in mind—whereby they might in some way secure an inside and important place in the direction of Japanese affairs. However, he was hopeful that they would finally accept our proposal if we stood firmly for it. He observed that the pattern of control which the Soviets had set in Hungary, Bulgaria, and Rumania was a pertinent precedent, though he assumed we would consult the Soviets in advance regarding any policy question.

Two brilliant members of the Embassy staff—George F. Kennan and John Paton Davies—were convinced that Soviet policy would be as geographically and politically revisionist in the Far East as in Eastern Europe, though tactically different because of the relative power situation in the two areas. Harriman also thought this probable. But he was inclined to wait for further evidence before renouncing hope it might be genuinely cooperative in regard to Japan.

All three were even then unsure of the reliability of Stalin's promise to refrain from aiding the Chinese Communists and from hindering Chiang Kai-shek's efforts to bring them within the loop of his authority. They all surmised that it was likely that if the Kuomintang Government faltered, and was ineffectual despite American support, the Soviet Government would find secret ways of maintaining helpful liaison with the Chinese Communists. The Soviet Government's efforts to nurture what it considered "friendly" governments in those Eastern European areas that were occupied by Soviet troops caused Harriman and his associates to anticipate possible similar attempts in Manchuria and North Korea—while Russian troops and commissars were there.

The first responses of our allies to our proposal that a Far Eastern Advisory Commission be formed were positive but qualified. The governments of the United Kingdom and Australia agreed to the constitution of an inter-Allied commission of the sort contemplated by Washington. But neither thought that the stated terms in mind would assure them either the fair or effective chance to influence policy which they believed they deserved—because of their part in the war against Japan and their wish for protection against possible future Japanese resurgence.

The Soviet Government (on either September 5 or September 7, a few days after MacArthur entered Japan) concurred in the proposal. But on doing so it stated the opinion that a Control Council was needed as well. This, it suggested, should have only four members—the representatives of the United States, the Soviet Union, Great Britain, and China.

Whether or not he grasped the earnestness of the British objections and the import of the Soviet suggestion, Byrnes decided to bring the large Advisory Commission into existence quickly. After it was started on its work, all the Allies, he thought, would be able to gauge more correctly whether changes in its authority and procedures were advisable, and the need for any other and smaller council such as the Soviet Union seemed to want.

The boldness with which MacArthur exercised his authority from the start was matched by the verve with which he talked about it. He quickly made known in a public statement his satisfaction that the Japanese Government was making every effort to execute the instructions in the surrender accord and to observe the orders which, at the Supreme Commander's behest, the Emperor and Government had issued. He then went on to state, "Therefore, at the present time, the Supreme

Commander for the Allied Powers is controlling the Government of Japan along the following lines"; and there followed an explanatory summary of the main elements of policy set down in the instrument of surrender and in the instructions that had been sent from Washington. But the language of the statement left the impression that he, the Supreme Commander, rather than the American or any foreign government, was author and arbiter of these policies. He was already intent on identifying the authority of the occupation with his office and himself, already diffusing the impression that it was he who determined policies.

MacArthur's statement evoked comment in the American press and discreet inquiries from foreign diplomats. Undersecretary of State Dean Acheson—Secretary of State Byrnes being in London at the first session of the Council of Foreign Ministers—undertook to clarify the relationship. Though it is only a surmise, it is a safe surmise that before doing so he informed President Truman of what he was going to say, and the President told him to go ahead. Acheson, whose nomination had not yet been confirmed by the Senate, was asked at a press conference whether he had any comments on MacArthur's statement. He answered, "The important thing is that the policy in regard to Japan is the same policy which has always been held by this Government and is still held so far as I know, and I think I know. In carrying out that policy, the occupation forces are the instruments of policy and not the determinants of policy, and the policy is and has been that the surrender of Japan will be carried out; that Japan will be put in a position where it cannot renew aggressive warfare; that the present economic and social system in Japan which makes for a will to war will be changed so that the will to war will not continue; and that whatever it takes to carry this out will be used to carry it out." [5]

[5] Acting Secretary Acheson's press and radio news conference, September 19, 1945 ("Concerning Occupation Force in Japan," The Department of State Bulletin, vol. XIII, No. 326, September 23, 1945, p. 427).

On September 21 Senator Kenneth S. Wherry wrote a letter to Acheson saying he was amazed to read of Acheson's rebuke to MacArthur and asking among other questions, "Is General MacArthur acting as representative only of the United States Government or of the Allied Governments as well in implementing the terms of the Potsdam agreement?" [6]

Acheson answered on September 22 merely by sending Wherry 1) a copy of his (Acheson's) press statement, 2) a copy of the Potsdam Declaration, and 3) a copy of the United States Initial Post-Surrender Policy for Japan.

Aware that the directive to MacArthur would surely become public knowledge, the State Department released its text. It was probably read intently by the assembled Council of Foreign Ministers in London, where Byrnes was already engaged in a confused squabble about every item on its program. Whether by coincidence or not, Molotov hastened to inform Byrnes more definitely of two important changes which the Soviet Government wanted in those arrangements which Byrnes had blithely proposed and briskly pushed.

[6] "Concerning Policy Toward Japan: Exchange of Letters Between Senator Wherry and Acting Secretary Acheson," The Department of State Bulletin, vol. XIII, No. 327, September 30, 1945, pp. 479–480.

IV

Stalemate at London

Japan was not even on the agenda of the five Foreign Ministers who met in London in that late September of 1945. But the question of how it was to be controlled during the occupation was thrust forward. Since it became connected with other issues, to grasp what happened, the span of our attention must stretch over wider areas of contention.

Three of the Foreign Ministers were veterans of the Potsdam Conference. Each had formed impressions of the tactics of the others. Byrnes knew Molotov to be a cold and hard negotiator who relied on stubbornness and tireless repetition to win acceptance of Russia's purposes. Molotov thought Byrnes an agile opponent of the Soviet Union, a cunning schemer for American capitalism. Ernest Bevin, the British Foreign Secretary, thought Molotov a malicious and determined enemy of the British Empire; and Molotov probably disliked him all the more because he was an independent labor leader and a patriotic socialist.

Byrnes and Bevin usually managed to stand together; they were looking in the same direction though from different angles. But they were not drawn personally to each other. To Bevin,

Byrnes may have seemed at times a pert, even cocky Irishman of the type he had known on the docks. To Byrnes, Bevin probably appeared at times unsubtle and fumbling.

In short, Molotov and the representatives of the West tended mutually to regard each other as advocates of national purposes rather than as partners in the pursuit of peace. Of the three, Molotov was the most certain of this. Communists are drilled to expel any thought of greater purposes from their interpretations of the acts of any and all opponents.

Along with these three there sat, as the representative of France, Georges Bidault, a combative person of narrow mentality and spirit. The Chinese representative, Wang Shih-chieh, was a discreet and quiet man. He strove to be conciliatory, since Chiang Kai-shek wanted to retain the support of the American Government without offending the Soviet Government.

The time between the conferences at Potsdam and at London—about six weeks—was so short that preparatory exchanges of views and proposals had been of necessity compressed. The state of Europe was ominously disturbed; war-damaged nations were staggering in distress; deprivation was general; civil strife was imminent in many countries. With the coming of winter the situation would become worse unless decisions were reached that ended quarrels, resolved uncertainties, and inaugurated measures which might start the nations back to health and stable order. Victory over Germany, the Western countries feared, might turn out to be merely a prelude to a further plunge into trouble, and Communist seizure of power.

The Soviet Government was not worried by such possible eventualities. The Soviet Union had been hard struck, but was larger than ever and proudly confident. Thus it reckoned that because of their anxiety the Western Allies might be readier to accede to Soviet terms and aspirations than they had been at Potsdam. Only the United States could afford to stand firm.

But craving the end of wartime sacrifices, it was bringing home its triumphant armies from Europe and Asia.

Conditions, thus, caused the Americans to wish to dispose of Conference questions quickly. Temperamentally also they were so inclined. Truman was impatient with the ordeal of long argument. Byrnes, as a former senator from South Carolina, had been habituated to the making of speedy deals in fractious and rule-bound legislative committees.

The quicker to get done with the long list of matters which were to be discussed, the members of the Council adopted Byrnes' proposal that on most days they should meet in both the morning and the afternoon. As a consequence everyone—and no one more than Byrnes—was always too busy. Neither he nor his advisers had enough chance between the formal sessions to talk over among themselves or with other members of the Council the many subjects which were considered. Consequently, much of the time of the Council was taken by long statements and arguments which might have been avoided by preliminary consultation. The morning meetings usually went on for almost three hours, the afternoon meetings for almost four hours. At the end of each day everyone was tired, even Molotov, accustomed as he was to the long discourses of Communist congregations.

On the agenda were most of the jolting issues which had been left unsettled at Potsdam. Enumeration must be left to those who tell the whole tale of this abortive London Conference. We need take into account only those few that were foremost in the minds of the chief negotiators, those to which the contest over the control of Japan became adjunct.

Each member of the Council had different primary aims.

The American Government wished most to arrive at agreement about the preparation and completion of the peace treaties for Italy, Rumania, Bulgaria, Hungary, and Finland.

The aims of the Soviet Government were quintuple.

While urging Great Britain to withdraw its forces from Greece, it sought recognition for the puppet regimes imposed on Rumania and Bulgaria. It was bidding for one of the Italian colonies in the eastern end of the Mediterranean and for control of the Dardanelles Straits, and was trying to detach part of Iran. It was insistent on securing huge reparations from Germany.

The stand of the British Government was self-preserving and defensive. It was determined not to be expelled from Greece. And it was firmly opposed to the attempted thrusts of Soviet imperialism into the eastern Mediterranean and to Soviet wishes to keep its forces in the northern section of Iran.

The desire of the French Government was concentrated on securing protection against a resurgence of Germany. To this end Bidault opposed all attempts to establish central administration for the whole of Germany. What he sought under orders from his President, General Charles de Gaulle, was an agreement to place the Ruhr industrial district under permanent international control and the Rhineland under an administration in which France might have the dominant influence. To foretell—Bidault and De Gaulle had to resign themselves, for the time being, to the deferment of their proposal. But the French desire to participate as an equal, from start to finish, in the making of all European peace treaties, was stoutly upheld by Byrnes and Bevin.

The Chinese Government shared the same wish to be present when the peace treaties were discussed. Its representative was there to guard China against any decision which might hurt or endanger it, rather than to advance new claims. Tacitly, he could be counted on to favor decisions which would retard the expansion of Communism.

On the advance program, no Far Eastern situation or issue was listed. None had been proposed. The American Government assumed it had the direction of Japan well in hand and arrangements for consultation with its allies well in mind and in train.

On the issue over which the Conference broke up—the procedure for arriving at European peace treaties—there was at the start no difference. As one follows the circuit of the argument, the surmise is generated that the real reason the dispute arose was that it became entangled with others— among them the contest over the control of Japan. These two questions were at the opposite ends of the tug between the West and the Soviet Union over areas or spheres of influence.

At the first meeting of the Council (September 11) Molotov agreed that all five members should be permitted to attend all of its meetings and participate in all of its discussions—no matter what subject was on the table. However, it was also understood that *only* the representatives of those governments which had been signatories to the capitulation of any country should have the right to *vote* on the terms of the peace treaty with that country.

The American delegation hastened to present a memo containing proposals about a peace treaty with Italy. Molotov submitted an offsetting one about peace treaties with Rumania and Bulgaria. These submissions were enlivened by Byrnes' critical comments about the situation in Bulgaria and Rumania and Molotov's rejoinder that the Western Allies were supporting an illegitimate and unrepresentative government in Greece.

The next few days went in a swirl of discussion about the disposition of the Italian colonies, the Yugoslav-Italian frontier, and Trieste. The Soviet position on these matters, taken in conjunction with its attempt to secure control of the Dardanelles Straits and its espousal of the Communist rebellion in Greece, worried the Western negotiators. How set were Soviet rulers on these aims? Were they absolute or were they being advanced mainly to create alarm and to dispose the Western Allies to accept Soviet domination of Southeastern Europe in return for relinquishment of its claims elsewhere? Such transactions were traditional in European conference diplomacy.

Despite these perplexities, some progress was made toward

agreement about the terms of the several peace treaties. On September 21, in connection with the resumption of discussion about the Bulgarian peace treaty, Byrnes once again said that the American Government would not recognize the existing governments in Rumania and Bulgaria because it did not believe them to be either representative or democratic. Molotov asserted that American policy had changed. He contended that Byrnes' remarks showed that the United States wanted to have governments in these countries which were unfriendly to the Soviet Union. Byrnes' rejoinder was that Stalin had made no objection when President Truman at Potsdam had taken the same position as he, Byrnes, was maintaining, and it was Molotov alone who was making this unfounded accusation. Molotov had snarled; Byrnes, the soft-spoken man from South Carolina, had bitten.

This, in most sketchy summary, was the state of the conference when, on September 22, the divergence between the American and Soviet Governments about the arrangements for the control of Japan came to the fore.

Molotov sent word to Byrnes that he would like to see him alone before the scheduled morning meeting of the conference. Greetings having been exchanged, Molotov, ignoring that fracas of the day before, said that he wanted to talk about Japan. He made no reference to the fact that the text of the directive to MacArthur had just been released for publication.[1]

His government, Molotov said, thought that the time had come to conclude a treaty directed against the renewal of Japanese aggression. It was, he added, all the more inclined to think so, in view of the manner in which the terms of sur-

[1] The text of the directive to MacArthur appeared in the London press on the morning of this day, September 22. No doubt it had been released shortly before. I have been unable to determine just when the text was received in Moscow—whether before or after the issuance of the instruction which, it can be assumed, was sent to Molotov and by which Molotov was guided in his talk with Byrnes.

render were being carried out. Byrnes answered merely that it was a matter that would have to be carefully considered.

Molotov then went on to say that the Soviet Government thought that a Control Council made up of the representatives of the four major Allies should be constituted for Japan—a Council which could supervise the execution of the terms of surrender. Of this idea Byrnes had, as has been mentioned, received previous notice. But possibly because he had not perceived that the Soviet Government would seriously pursue it, he had let it rest. Now, after remarking that the subject was not on the program of this conference, he told Molotov that before stating its views the American Government would want to consult the Supreme Commander, and therefore he could not discuss it then and there. However, he promised that he would raise the question as soon as he got back to Washington and let Molotov know as soon as he could what the American Government thought.

Molotov then showed that he had more faith in Soviet power to obstruct American wishes than in the American disposition to satisfy Soviet wishes. Up to then the French and Chinese members had been allowed to state their views whenever the terms of one or another of the European treaties were being examined. For example, Wang Shih-chieh had presided over a long session in which agreement had been raised about various important elements in the peace treaty with Italy. But now Molotov retracted the assent he had given at the first session of the conference to the attendance of the French and Chinese Foreign Ministers at all meetings. He said that he thought a grave mistake had been made in allowing them to be present when matters with which they were not closely concerned were being discussed. He averred that the Potsdam Agreement had contemplated that the three governments—the American, Soviet, and British—and they alone, should engage in the making of the five European peace treaties under consideration. The Soviet Government, he asserted, was willing to have Bidault continue to participate in the talks about the

Italian peace treaty but not in those about the other treaties. And it thought that since these treaties were none of China's business, Wang Shih-chieh should absent himself when any or all of them were being determined.

At this juncture Bevin joined Byrnes and Molotov.[2] He was as upset as Byrnes. He argued that while the Potsdam Agreement did not explicitly grant France and China the right to vote on the terms of peace with the countries with whom they had not signed armistice terms, they ought to be enabled, under a broad construction of the agreement, to be present during the discussion of these treaties, and to express their views. If they were not, he continued, they would be resentful and their ill will would harm all the work of this conference. But Molotov stubbornly maintained that the position he now held was clearly in accord with the Potsdam Agreement; that an error had been made, which should be corrected; and that the Agreement must be faithfully observed.[3]

Still at odds, the three Foreign Ministers drove over to the conference hall. There, as soon as all members of the Council had taken their places, Molotov repeated what he had told Byrnes and Bevin. The French and Chinese members were shocked. Bidault was so angry that he seemed about to walk out of the Council and issue a public statement. But Byrnes and Bevin persuaded him to wait a while.

[2] Desmond Donnelly in his book *The Cold War*, New York, St. Martin's Press, 1965, pp. 206–207, gives an account of this conversation which, it may be guessed, was relayed to him by Bevin.

[3] The pertinent provisions of the Potsdam Agreement are in Section I of the *Protocol of Proceedings of the Berlin Conference*, concerning the "Establishment of a Council of Foreign Ministers," and Section IX, "Conclusion of Peace Treaties and Admission to the United Nations Organization."

These assigned the task of treaty-making only and jointly to the three powers, except that in the case of the Italian treaty France was also to be included. However, they also stipulated that "other members will be invited to participate when matters directly concerning them are under discussion."

It was either at this session or at one of those held on the next day, September 23, that Molotov said that if the Soviet Government took back its assent to the presence of the French and Chinese representatives when treaties were discussed, the earlier agreement was no longer in point. Bevin commented that this had also been Hitler's way. Molotov turned to Byrnes, who was in the chair, and said, "Have we no Chairman to protect members from insults?" He started to walk out of the room. Before he reached the door Bevin said he would retract his remark. He apologized and Molotov returned to his seat.

Byrnes asked President Truman to help avert the breakup of the conference. As recounted by the President,[4]

> I was spending a brief weekend at Jefferson Island in Chesapeake Bay when I received a message from Admiral Leahy through the code room aboard the *Williamsburg*. The admiral had just held a teletype conversation with Secretary Byrnes in London during which the Secretary of State reported that . . . Molotov declared that he would attend no further meetings unless France and China were excluded from all matters where they were not directly concerned as signatories of an armistice agreement. Byrnes believed this to be only an excuse for Molotov to leave the conference and that the fact was that he was angry because the United States and Britain would not recognize Rumania [the government in power in Rumania]. Byrnes suggested that I wire Stalin immediately, asking him to communicate with Molotov and not allow the Council to be broken up. Since I was en route to the *Williamsburg* at the time the teletype conversation took place, Byrnes and Leahy, realizing that the situation could not wait until my arrival at the ship, took

[4] *Year of Decisions*, pp. 516–518.

39

the unusual step of anticipating my approval and agreed on a message to be sent to Stalin in my name. This read as follows:

"I am informed that Mr. Molotov is considering withdrawing from the Council of Foreign Ministers in London because of difficulty in reaching agreement as to the participation of France and China in discussions of the Balkan situation [*sic*].

"I urgently request that you communicate with Mr. Molotov telling him that because of the bad effect it would have on world peace he should not permit the Council to be broken up."

Leahy had another teletype conversation with London in which Byrnes suggested a more personal presentation. So the President quickly sent a second message to Stalin:

The Secretary of State has fully informed me of the difficulty encountered at the Council of Foreign Ministers.

I agree that under a strict interpretation of the language of the Potsdam Agreement, France and China have not the right to participate in the construction of peace treaties unless they are signatories to the surrender terms or unless they are invited under paragraph 3(2) of the Potsdam Agreement which provides that members of the Council other than the signatories may by agreement be invited to participate when matters directly concerning them are under discussion.

It is my recollection that at the conference table at Potsdam it was agreed during the discussion that members not signatory could be present and participate in the discussion but could not vote. It seems the first day the Council met, it was unanimously agreed that members not signatories could participate in the discussion, but could not vote. If we now change this rule and deny France and China because they are not signatories to the surrender the right even to discuss a matter in which they state they are interested, I fear it will create a bad impression. It will be charged that the three big powers are denying other members of the Council an opportunity even to present their views.

Can't we agree to regard the unanimous action of the Council on the opening day as an invitation to France and China to participate under the Potsdam Agreement? This is too small a matter to disrupt the work of the Council and delay progress toward peace and better understanding.

Attlee made a similar appeal to Stalin.

But the Marshal was unmoved. His reply to Truman on September 24 was stiff:

I have received your second message regarding the Council of Ministers.

I have received today a reply from Mr. V. M. Molotov who informed me that he is acting in accordance with the decision of the Berlin Conference and considers that this decision should not be violated. On my part, I have to remind you that at the Berlin Conference neither a decision was adopted nor was it agreed among us that the members of the Council who did not sign the terms of surrender could participate in the discussions but could not vote. I consider that the position of Molotov to adhere strictly to the decision of the Berlin Conference cannot make a bad impression and should not offend anybody.

It will have been noted that Byrnes and Bevin attributed the change in the Soviet position about treaty procedure to displeasure over their refusal to recognize the regimes in power in Rumania (and Bulgaria). Neither then nor later did Molotov or Stalin explicitly connect it with any other subject under discussion. But conjunction of time and circumstance suggests that it was activated in part also by Byrnes' slide past the Soviet proposal for a Control Council for Japan.

For Molotov went on to test the possibilities of securing immediate consideration of that proposal. At the next session of the conference (on September 24) he submitted a memo in which he again advanced the request. In response, Byrnes repeated the reasons why he could not discuss it then and there. The American Government needed time to consider whether it would be helpful, and it could not give a conclusive answer until it had consulted with MacArthur.

Answers which President Truman gave to questions asked of him at a press conference soon thereafter admitted no ground for Soviet complaints. He was dismissive. Questioned about the Soviet proposal to establish an Allied Control Council for Japan, the President said that the establishment of the Japanese Government (*sic*) had been agreed to by all the Allied powers and that he had not received notice that it was unsatisfactory to any of them. When asked further about reports that the Russians were trying to create an Allied Control Council, he said that he had no comment, adding that all he knew was what he read in the newspapers.[5] If he had been informed that the Soviet Government had made a similar suggestion when agreeing to the formation of the Far Eastern Advisory Commission, he had probably forgotten.

The press correspondents persisted. Recalling that the statement which the White House had issued on Japan had

[5] As reported by the New York *Herald Tribune* of September 27, 1945, in a front page article headed "Truman is Cool to Russian Bid on Japan Rule."

asserted that if the principal Allied powers differed, American policies would govern, they asked whether there was any regular channel through which the Allies could make their opinions known.[6] Truman's answer took much for granted. He said that all the interested powers had concurred in the appointment of MacArthur, and he had been designated to act for all of them. Our Allies, he continued, could express their opinions on the occupation through the Joint (presumably Combined) Chiefs of Staff. Then, being asked how the Russians could do that since they did not have any members on the Combined Chiefs of Staff, he said that the Russians had representatives with General MacArthur and that they could also express their views through the White House. He repeated that the Russians had never expressed any dissatisfaction with the occupation. Was this a lapse in Byrnes' reporting or a lapse in Truman's memory?

Acheson was less peremptory. Asked whether the statement issued by the White House on Japanese policy had been submitted to our Allies before it was given to General MacArthur, Acheson stated that he believed that it had been transmitted to our Allies. When further asked whether this was merely a unilateral declaration, Acheson said that it was a statement of United States Government policy; that the situation in Japan was one which had to go forward and in which things had to get done and that had made the issuance of the White House statement essential. He went on to say that the American Government had to use the best means of consultation that could be worked out pending the establishment of regular machinery for consultation. He repeated that the Allies had accepted MacArthur as Supreme Commander and that he had to deal with matters all the time, to go on and do things, but there was no disposition on the part of the American Government to exclude anybody.

[6] Presumably this is a reference to a paragraph in Part II, "Allied Authority," in the *United States Initial Post-Surrender Policy for Japan.*

43

The appeals to Stalin having failed, subsequent talks wrought no change in the Soviet contentions about the disputed matters before the Conference.

Byrnes (on September 26) tried to persuade Molotov to accept an amended plan of procedure for peace-making. This deferred to Soviet preference that only those countries which had signed the armistice with a particular enemy state should prepare the preliminary text of the peace treaty with that state. But it contemplated that subsequently there would be a conference in which other states that had been at war against the Axis should have their chance to have a say. Molotov turned this down.

Then Byrnes, in a last-minute effort to save the conference, proposed that there be still a third stage in the procedure of treaty-making: ". . . that after full and free discussion by the invited states the final approval of the terms of the treaty of peace will be made by those . . . states which were at war with the enemy states in question." But Molotov rejected this proposal also. He stood hard and fast on the Soviet interpretation of the Potsdam Agreement.

Harriman attributed this rigidity primarily to American refusal to recognize the existing governments in Bulgaria and Rumania, and to a fear of being overruled on this issue. But still, with his talk with Stalin alive in his memory, the Ambassador thought that the Soviet Government might also be trying by its stubbornness—which was delaying the peace treaty with Italy eagerly desired by the United States—to cause us to be more regardful of its wish to share in the control of Japan.

So he besought Byrnes to make more of an effort to placate Moscow without depriving the United States of adequate powers of decision or permitting purposeful interference with MacArthur's control and direction of the occupation. If we paid heed to Russia's interest in Japan, the Ambassador thought, Molotov would be less able to use this issue to divert attention from the Soviet insistence upon retaining dominant control over the governments of Eastern Europe. He feared that we were unnecessarily arousing Soviet suspicions, which would affect their policies in other Far Eastern matters, especially as regards taking their troops out of Manchuria.

He forecast that the Soviet Government would not be satisfied unless it was agreed to establish some sort of Control Council; and he suggested that this Council might follow the pattern of those that were operative in Hungary, Bulgaria, and Rumania. General MacArthur as Supreme Commander would retain ultimate power of decision and be obligated only to consult with other members of the Control Council on matters of policy. The American Government, he thought, would be well advised to act quickly and voluntarily rather than appear to be forced unwillingly into acceding to Soviet wishes in order to avert other troubles in the Far East.

Byrnes felt that he could not try out this direct line before he had consulted with President Truman and General MacArthur. But he thought he saw a chance to try a more indirect one.

Up to then the British Government had been withholding its final assent to the American proposal for a Far Eastern Advisory Commission (FEAC). It wished the role of the Commission to be enlarged. Moreover, as Bevin had told Byrnes, the British Cabinet favored the Soviet idea that there should be a four-power Control Council as well. But on September 29 the British Foreign Secretary informed Byrnes that the British Government would cooperate in the creation of the FEAC, with the expectation that the American Government would support two relatively minor amendments. Byrnes promised to do so. Thereupon he proceeded to announce publicly that the American, Russian, British, and Chinese Governments had agreed to the establishment of an Advisory Commission of all governments which had a primary interest in the development of policy for Japan. With the hope that this might satisfy the

Soviet Government and relieve the jam in the Conference of Foreign Ministers in London, the announcement further stated that "The Far Eastern Advisory Commission will also be asked to consider whether a Control Council should be established and, if so, what powers should be vested in it."

In an effort to persuade Molotov to be content with this possibility for the present, Byrnes wrote him a long explanatory letter. In this, after restating the terms of reference for the Far Eastern Advisory Commission—embodying various changes that had been agreed on—he said that as soon as he got back to Washington he would ask the President to instruct the American representative on the Commission to urge immediate consideration of whether a Control Council should be established, and if so, what powers were to be vested in it. The letter ended with an expression of hope that the Soviet Government would name its representative to the Commission as soon as possible so that it might begin its work at once.

Molotov hastened to contradict Byrnes' public announcement. The Moscow radio broadcast as a Tass Agency dispatch from London the substance of the reply which he sent Byrnes on October 1. In this he said the earlier Soviet assent to the original American proposal to create an Advisory Commission did not accurately reflect "the present situation." For, he continued, the formation of this Commission had been delayed, and subsequently the Soviet Government had proposed that there be also a Control Council—to meet in Tokyo—to consist of the representatives of the four main powers, of which the American member would be the president.

Molotov explained that in the opinion of the Soviet Government, as long as a war situation had existed and the Japanese forces were still not disarmed, there was justification for concentrating all functions for the control of Japan in the hands of the Supreme Commander. That period was past; henceforth the questions to be decided would be chiefly political, economic, and financial; and the Soviet Government believed these should be considered in an Allied agency through which the four powers who had played a decisive role in defeating Japan could effectuate policies reached by agreement and assume joint responsibility for them. Finally, the Soviet Government thought that the larger Far Eastern Advisory Commission should not be formed *until* the four powers had decided to establish the Control Council, since delay in doing so "would create appreciable difficulties." Molotov did not explain what difficulties he had in mind. It could not be foretold whether he meant merely that the Soviet Government would refuse to join the Advisory Commission, or whether it would try to make trouble for the United States and its allies in China and Japan. Negotiations in the conference about other issues were at a stop. Molotov's reply to the American proposal about Japan ended the last perceptible hope and chance of getting them going again.

Wang Shih-chieh had striven to keep the London Conference going, to keep its members talking. Byrnes got the impression that the Russians were trying to delay the end until he (Byrnes) should be in the chair. Helpfully, the Chinese Minister said he would bear the onus of moving the adjournment on the afternoon of October 2, when he would be presiding. At that session Molotov entered the room smiling, and said in jest he had a suggestion to make to the other members. "If you want to surrender today, I will be ready to discuss the questions you want to talk about tomorrow." Byrnes remarked that he thought Molotov had to consult his government in person. Molotov replied that he was in contact with his government every day. Byrnes thereupon challenged him by asking whether on the morrow he would be willing to discuss the questions at issue in the group of five—that is, in the presence of the French and Chinese members. "No," said Molotov, "I stand on the Potsdam Declaration."

Wang thereupon concluded that no good could come of permitting this quarrelsome exchange to go on into the late evening hours. He said, "It is I who suggested that you wait here for two days before ending this conference, but I gather that no one has anything more to say." Pausing long enough to be polite, he thereupon said, "I declare the meeting adjourned." So it was—without setting any time for resumption.

The note of geniality on which the London Conference had begun, seeped out of it toward the end. Bevin, in contrast to his predecessor, Sir Anthony Eden, who had remained suave and conciliatory in similar conferences, spoke to the Russians bluntly and sometimes gruffly. Molotov was his usual ungiving self. The way in which Byrnes and Bevin stood up to him caused him to become more fractious and to make unfair statements about American policies and intentions. These Byrnes resented. The Secretary of State, instead of reiterating, as American representatives at other conferences so often had, how much we valued Russian friendship, met Russian claims and assertions head on. But even as he did, he sought possible compromises and genuinely regretted that acceptable ones did not emerge.

At dinner with Harriman before his departure from London, Byrnes told the Ambassador that it was now up to him to straighten out the situation after he returned to Moscow. Harriman suggested that in due course the President send him a message to be delivered personally to Stalin. Then perhaps he could ascertain from Stalin himself what basically was disturbing him. Whether or not he could bring Stalin to grasp and fairly judge the American point of view about the main questions that seemed to have caused the break, he could tell only after trying. Byrnes said he would wait and see and talk the situation over with the President.

In an informative radio broadcast Byrnes gave on October 5, three days after the end of the conference, he emphasized that the issue which had disrupted the conference was, in his view, not trivial or merely technical—that of the procedure for making the European treaties. "It presented an issue which had to be met," he said. "It is whether the peace shall be made by three or even five nations to the exclusion of other nations vitally concerned in the maintenance and enforcement of the peace. . . ." In his opinion the view that a few powerful governments should, by and of themselves, determine terms of peace and tell others to "sign on the dotted line" was unfair and would not make for lasting settlements. In upholding this view, the American Government probably discerned possible advantage. But it was in accord with the then prevalent conception that international settlements should be developed by discussions of the whole interested society of nations—as in the United Nations—rather than determined by confined negotiations, since these usually turned into a barter of segments or spheres of influence or power.

If the United States had been charged with inconsistency in its determination to retain the ruling voice in Japan, Byrnes probably would have argued that membership in the Far Eastern Advisory Commission would accord all countries closely concerned ample chance to share in the formulation of policies for Japan and the terms accorded it.

Although in their public utterances all the principal participants in the London Conference avowed the belief that the differences between them would be adjusted and that their collaboration would continue, the impression left was somber, if not ominous. But a swift ruffle through the clippings of American newspapers has turned up one commentator who, if not satisfied with the outcome, was not disturbed by it. This was John Foster Dulles, another of Byrnes' advisers. He was widely reported as believing that since all governments had made their views clear and the American negotiators had not sought a paper victory by concessions, the session had given the five powers a firm foundation on which to build. The correspondent to whom he spoke over the telephone reported him as saying that "a long talk with Viacheslav M. Molotov, Soviet Foreign Commissar, led to the conviction that Soviet-American relations are better than ever." [7]

It is to be remarked that neither the American nor the Soviet officials referred in their public utterances to the talks that had occurred between Byrnes and Molotov about the Soviet proposal for the establishment of a Control Council in Japan. It may be that Soviet official reticence led Byrnes to continue to believe that this question would yield to deft handling; that if the American Government hurried on with its own plans, the Soviet Government would not take its action too greatly amiss, and would be no more arbitrary about other matters at issue than it would have been in any event.

[7] As reported by Bert Andrews in the New York *Herald Tribune*, October 3, 1945, in a story headed "Dulles Cheerful, Says 5 Powers Got One Another's Real Views," pp. 1–2, and by the Washington correspondent of the London *Times*, in the issue of October 4, 1945, "Mr. Dulles' Hopeful Account."

V

Interim Responses

So the Secretary of State went ahead. He called the Far Eastern Advisory Commission into existence before giving any conclusive answer to the Soviet proposal for an Allied Control Council, even as the Soviet Union was going ahead in Central Europe.

On October 6 all those governments which had responded to the original proposal for an Advisory Commission, including the Soviet Government, were invited to attend a first meeting of the Commission. This was to be held in Washington on October 23. Let the Soviet Government make up its mind whether to have a representative present, or to have him stay away!

Concurrently, work was begun on a message from the President to Stalin, designed to break the impasse. Before leaving London, Harriman and Assistant Secretary of State James C. Dunn had written and submitted a draft to Byrnes. It was conciliatory in tone. But George Kennan, who was in temporary charge of the Moscow Embassy, on learning of this contemplated step, sent a message to Harriman saying he thought it would be a great tactical mistake to approach Stalin at this juncture. In his opinion it would be wiser to be quiescent for a while, rather than to hurry to approach Stalin with new requests or proposals. For if we did, Kennan thought, the Soviet rulers would conclude that the American Government was worried. If they continued to be inflexible their view would prevail, and those officials who encouraged Molotov to be stubborn would be proven right. A good chance to discredit the tougher element in the Kremlin would be lost.

When on October 10 it was announced that Stalin had gone on vacation "for a rest," Harriman wondered whether the Kremlin was trying the same tactics—in obverse. For never before had Stalin's movements been reported in the press and the Soviet people been told that he needed a rest.

While decision regarding the dispatch of the message to Stalin was in suspense, Byrnes gave the press full information about the original (August 21) American proposal for an Advisory Commission. At a press conference on October 10, he told of the acceptance by the Soviet, Chinese, and British Governments, and of the requests with which the British Government had accompanied its hesitant acceptance. He announced that all had been asked to come to its first meeting, on October 23. He mentioned that the Soviet Foreign Commissar, Molotov, was maintaining that the establishment of this FEAC should be preceded by formation of a Control Council. What to do about that, he commented, the President and the Joint Chiefs of Staff would decide, but he, himself, did not think it advisable. The FEAC, Byrnes thought, could provide adequate opportunities for all to know what was being done in Japan, and to cooperate in its administration. For the Commission, he explained, would be authorized to recommend long-term policies for Japan; and the member governments could, in consultation, determine how to carry them out and whether any other organization was needed. The Commission could also consider to what further extent other governments should participate in arrangements for and direction of the occupation.

On October 12 (Moscow time) Molotov notified Harriman that for reasons he had explained in London, the Soviet

Government could not agree to the formation of the FEAC prior to the creation of a Control Council. Before Harriman's report of his talk was received, the Secretary of State had sent the Ambassador the text of the message from Truman to Stalin which Harriman was to deliver in person. It was earnest in its professions of a wish to concert our policy with that of the Soviet Union. However, it dealt only with the question of procedure for treaty-making and the reform of the governments of Rumania and Bulgaria. It was essentially an appeal for Soviet acquiescence in the proposals Byrnes had made in a final effort to reach agreement at London.[1]

When Harriman told Molotov that the President wished him to deliver this message to Stalin so that he might explain and discuss it, Molotov said that the Marshal was on vacation at Sochi, in the Caucasus area of the Black Sea, and would not be returning to Moscow for a month and a half. He offered to send the message to Stalin. Harriman said that he knew that Stalin was on holiday but still hoped that he could receive him since the subject of the message was so important. Molotov promised to inform Stalin of Harriman's request. In reporting this conversation with Molotov, Harriman told Byrnes that he foresaw that when and as he met Stalin, the Marshal would certainly raise the question of the arrangements for the control of Japan, ignored in the President's plea.

On being told of the message which Truman had instructed Harriman to deliver to Stalin, Bevin said it was all right. However, he thought that to approach the Soviet Government so

---

[1] Byrnes, it will be recalled, had then said that he would reluctantly assent to the restricted participation in the preparation of the peace treaties provided that thereafter all the principally interested states (all permanent members of the U.N. Security Council, all European members of the U.N., and those non-European members of the U.N. which had supplied substantial armed contingents in the war against European members of the Axis) would have the chance, in conference, to express their views about the proposed treaties before the final decisions were made by the small inner group.

quickly about this issue of peace-treaty procedure was a blunder and suggested that no move be made until Stalin returned to Moscow. Moreover, Bevin said he assumed that Truman's message would not commit the British Government, and that if Stalin should respond favorably the American Government would then consult not only with the British Government but with the governments of France and China.

On October 18 Molotov advised Harriman that Stalin had sent word that he would ". . . receive Ambassador Harriman with pleasure at Sochi where I am on vacation in order to receive President Truman's message and discuss it with the Ambassador. I suggest that the visit take place on October 24, 25 or 26." Harriman said the sooner the better. He and Molotov settled on the twenty-fourth.

In the interval before Harriman went down to Sochi, in a personal letter to Acheson, he stressed the need to remain mindful of the situation in China. He recommended that we aid the Chinese National Government to equip and train its armies, and give it prompt and vigorous economic aid. For he predicted that unless a sufficient and well-qualified Chinese force was ready to take over Manchuria when the Soviet army was to depart three months after the end of hostilities, the Soviet forces would not be evacuated. In other words, the possibility was beginning to loom up that the Communists—Chinese or Russian or both—would obtain or retain control of Manchuria and North China.

Harriman urgently sought to find out what he might say to Stalin about the arrangements for the control of Japan.

In one of several messages to Washington on this subject (the one sent on October 16), Harriman had set down his surmises about Stalin's view of the development of the question. He specified the points which he anticipated Stalin would make—and to which he, Harriman, would have to be able to give satisfactory answers or explanations if Stalin's suspicions were to be allayed. Because this message brought clearer comprehension in Washington, and because it so clearly identified the issues that had to be settled, its main items may be noted.

Harriman said 1) that he knew how blunt and direct Stalin had always been in his talks and that he thought Stalin would argue that we had invited the Soviet Union to come into the war against Japan but it was now being excluded from appropriate consideration in dealing with defeated Japan; 2) that Stalin would not consider membership in the FEAC sufficient participation for the Soviet Government; 3) that Stalin will feel that, in sending out invitations for the first meeting of the FEAC, the American Government had disregarded Molotov's request that it should be agreed to establish a Control Council *before* the FEAC meeting; 4) that he, Harriman, fully concurred in the decision that MacArthur as Supreme Commander must have final authority; but he had assumed that we were disposed to consult fully with our allies, keep them fully informed, and try to reach agreement on policies, and that we would take independent action only if agreement proved impossible; 5) that our proposal to discuss a Control Council in the FEAC would be deemed unsatisfactory, because Stalin believed that such a fundamental subject could be discussed frankly and fully only in a smaller group.

Did the American Government, he went on to inquire, intend to go ahead with the meeting of October 23, even though the Soviet Government did not accept membership? Or did it intend to have any more discussions, formal or informal, with the Soviet Government in the week remaining before the FEAC met?

He said he felt it would be better to present our position to Stalin frankly and try to get his general assent and if possible avoid the deepening of an impasse. He suggested that in this way we stood the best chance of allaying Stalin's suspicions, which were evidently growing. Harriman recalled that Stalin had told Soong that China and Russia should realize that the United States might well be weak in her policies toward Japan and eventually become unconcerned, whereas Russia and China had a vital and continuing interest in eliminating Japan as a threat for the future.

Byrnes, as has been mentioned, had intended to proceed with the formation of the Far Eastern Advisory Commission even if the Soviet Union remained away. But when the Chinese Ambassador in Washington said that his government was uneasy about going ahead, he agreed that the first meeting, scheduled for October 23, might be postponed to the thirtieth. Perhaps he did so the more readily because of the impress of Harriman's messages, and the hope that Harriman might be able to persuade Stalin of the genuineness of the value of membership on the Commission. In any event, circular notices of the postponement were dispatched.

Harriman advised Molotov of the postponement. Molotov's acknowledgment (on October 21) was supplemented by an exposition of Soviet ideas about the Control Council. This said that the Soviet Government, in proposing the formation of a control organ for Japan of the four Allied powers, did not intend that it should be analogous to the one in Germany, where there was no government. It thought rather that the Council in Japan should operate on a basis analogous to, for example, the Allied Control Commission for Rumania; as such it would operate under the direction of the American representative but the other members would enjoy the same rights and authority as the members of the Control Commission in Rumania.

This indicated the area of a compromise, but only hazily, because the realities of the Rumanian precedent were in dispute. It was not clear whether by citing it the Soviet Government was offering to forego the right to veto or unduly delay decision. An intent may be discerned of desire to find the basis for an accord in which the Soviet Union yielded primacy to the United States in Japan to the extent to which it obtained primacy in the direction of affairs in Eastern and Southeastern Europe. While the American Government did not think these situations were related, the Soviet Government would persist in connecting them in the scales of diplomacy.

Byrnes' response, of October 20, to Harriman's request for instructions also indicated new chances for a compromise. He said that, as he had promised Molotov, he had presented the views and ideas of the Soviet Government to President Truman. The American Government could not, Byrnes continued, assent to the substitution of a Control Council for the Supreme Commander. But—and he inched toward the Soviet ideas—he thought that a four-power Allied Military Council composed of representatives of each government whose forces participated in the Army of Occupation might be established *under* the Supreme Commander. This would be an executive council through which Allied decisions would be carried out; but in case of a difference of views in the Council, the decision of the Supreme Commander would prevail. General directives and political guidance forwarded to the Supreme Commander by the American Government would be submitted by him to the Council for consideration of the ways in which they were to be put into effect.

Byrnes also informed Harriman that the American Government intended to propose that the Soviet Union, the United Kingdom, and China would each provide thirty thousand men for the occupation army—all to be integrated with American forces under General MacArthur.

Harriman was briefly buoyed up because he thought the latest Soviet and American proposals might be near concordance.

He informed Byrnes that he was going to do his best to get Stalin to agree to send a Soviet representative to the first meeting of the FEAC, on October 30. He thought that as Molotov seemed to be climbing down, Stalin might agree to our request—particularly if he was authorized to tell him that Molotov's proposal (about the Council) was in principle acceptable and that the American Government was disposed to discuss it further in direct talks with the Soviet Government as well as in the Advisory Commission.

But hardly had this message left the Embassy in Moscow, when another one from Byrnes was decoded. The Secretary said he thought it best that Harriman should not discuss the proposed Allied Military Council with Stalin. General MacArthur was objecting to some of its features. The State Department thought this was due in part to his misunderstanding, and in part to the fact that its details had not been adequately clarified. MacArthur was disturbed lest the plan diminish his authority and feared that the other representatives on the Council would raise political and economic questions which should be settled elsewhere. Byrnes said that the discussions with MacArthur and the War Department would be pursued urgently.[2] For the time being all that Harriman had better say to Stalin was that he, Byrnes, was trying to satisfy Soviet wishes. This might be done by devising some sort of plan for implementing policy under the Supreme Commander either through the creation of some new council or through some change in the Advisory Commission, and he hoped to pursue the matter directly with the Soviet Government very soon.

This made it inevitable that Harriman's talk with Stalin should be at best only a transit toward an accord and not the end of the contest.

[2] Truman as well as Byrnes was becoming acquainted with MacArthur's inclination to be his own master. In *Year of Decisions* (pp. 519–520) he tells of a report which Edwin A. Locke, Jr., whom he had sent to China on a mission, wrote him about MacArthur's frame of mind. Locke said that MacArthur ". . . mentioned several times his difficulty in obtaining what he felt were prompt and understanding responses to cabled messages sent to Washington by the Supreme Allied Command." Truman goes on to say that "The general also told Locke that, in his opinion, policies relative to the control of Japan should for the most part be made in Tokyo rather than in Washington. The general 'spoke feelingly' of the problems created for him by policy pronouncements made in Washington without prior consultation with him."

VI

Harriman Talks with Stalin

At Sochi Harriman was housed in a villa where Lavrenti Beria, the former dreaded head of the Soviet secret police, had lived. It is, I believe, still in use as a guesthouse; in Russia the presence of ghosts does not cause houses to stay untenanted; non-persons have non-ghosts.

Stalin was cordial and seemed relaxed. Harriman's inclination to get down to business was as positive as his own. He gave Stalin a Russian translation of Truman's message, which was, it will be recalled, concerned only with the disagreement about recognition of the governments of Rumania and Bulgaria and the procedures for conceiving the peace treaties with Italy and the Balkan countries. Harriman's visit, the President said, provided a good chance for thrashing out these questions. He, Truman, was sure Stalin would agree with him "that the common interests of both our countries in the peace are far more important than any possible differences among us." [1] True, supremely true, and yet what fee, in power or influence, would be paid to keep the peace!

After reading the message Stalin looked up, and remarked

[1] This message is in *Stalin's Correspondence with Churchill, Attlee, Roosevelt and Truman*, Vol. II, New York, E. P. Dutton & Co., 1948, pp. 274–276.

that the Japanese question was not mentioned. Harriman parried, saying that it was under consideration between the State and War Departments and General MacArthur and that President Truman hoped to have some definite proposal by October 30, when the Advisory Commission would meet. But, Harriman continued, if Stalin would permit him to talk informally and regard what he said merely as his personal views and impressions, he would do his best to explain what the President and his advisers were thinking. Stalin said he would be glad if the Ambassador did.

Harriman then gave a lucid summary of the tenor of American official thought about Japan. He stressed our inclination to keep our allies informed and consult them rather than our determination that, when all was said and assessed, American views and purposes should prevail. But he did not screen that fact. Harriman's review of the past was preface to assurances that if Stalin sent a representative to the coming meeting of the Advisory Commission in Washington, he would find Byrnes ready to talk out the subject with him and desirous of reaching an agreement. The arrangement Byrnes would then propose, he surmised, would not be very different from the one which Molotov had recently outlined. The Advisory Commission would deal with all political and economic questions regarding Japan. Additionally, Washington was considering the constitution of an Allied Military Council, made up of the commanding generals of the national troop contingents which would be asked to join the occupation, all to be under the orders of the Supreme Command. This Council would be kept fully informed on all matters concerning Japan and would be able to discuss them all. Agreement would be sought—but it was to be understood that if not reached, MacArthur would have the final say.

Stalin's first comment was by analogy, the same analogy which Molotov had drawn. He referred to the Control Councils which were operative in Hungary and Rumania. As he described them, in these countries the Soviet Commander retained the ultimate right of decision, though perhaps not so complete as that sought for MacArthur. He, Stalin, took it for granted that in Japan the American representative, Mac-Arthur, should be permanent chairman of the Control Council and have the deciding voice. But, he continued—as if thinking aloud—if there were troops of other nationalities in Japan as there were in Germany, the rights of General MacArthur would in effect be restricted in some ways and measure. Therefore, he wondered whether it might not be inadvisable to have other troop contingents than American in Japan? That seemed to him more logical.

The historian is left to ramble among conjectures about the intent and import of this observation—whether it was simple or subtle. Was Stalin, exceptionally, just puzzled? Did it derive mainly from disinclination to have Soviet troops take orders from MacArthur and prevision that this might cause trouble? Or was it a way of ascertaining whether refusal to send Soviet troops might create anxiety in Washington and sway the American Government? Or—and I believe this the more probable—was Stalin testing the possibility of inducing the American Government to desist from opposing Soviet dominance in Rumania and Bulgaria, and perhaps elsewhere in the region, in return for acquiescence in American domination in Japan?

Stalin explicitly told Harriman the next day that he thought the two questions should be settled at the same time since they were linked. Stalin must have known how little influence the American and British members of the Control Council in the Southeastern European countries had been able to exert, how little they had been able to change or restrain Soviet exercise of control. Almost certainly he inferred that the proffered chance to know about and discuss what was done in Japan would not enable him effectively to advance the Communist cause in Japan.

To return from conjecture to narrative—the talk between Stalin and Harriman glided back to Truman's message. It reverted to the disputed questions of procedure for the making of the peace treaties. About the sprays of this talk, I will leave others to tell. Stalin favored five separate peace conferences, rather than one, each limited to those countries which had played a vital part in the fight against that former enemy, and those which had a vital interest in the treaty. Harriman expounded Truman's view that it had been all one war, that all of the former enemy states had helped Germany, and that it would be unfair and offensive to exclude any genuine participants. Stalin questioned particularly whether China, just because it was a member of the Security Council of the United Nations, should be permitted to attend the peace conferences for European countries, and doubted the justification for the presence of India, since it was distant and in reality ruled by Britain. He remarked that if it was an indivisible war, then Yugoslavia and Czechoslovakia, for example, should be invited to join in the discussion about Far Eastern affairs. This first talk on these matters was a standoff. But it did reveal more clearly than before the pros and cons of the American and Soviet opinions and indicated more clearly than before the lines of possible adjustment.

The talk on the second day was largely repetitive of what had been said on the first one. But it brought forth stronger and more precise complaints. It revealed how compatible in Stalin's mind—or companionate in his diplomatic reckoning— were the terms of accord about the control of the occupation of Japan and those about control over the countries of Southeastern Europe.

When Harriman renewed his request that Stalin send a representative to the prospective meeting of the Advisory Commission, to discuss whether or not a Military Council should also be formed, Stalin said he would rather not do so. The time had come, he thought, to establish a Control Council. This might be set up through direct discussions between the American and Soviet Governments; open discussions in the large Advisory Commission would be useless and cause trouble.

In a tone of mild indignation he gave reasons for his refusal to be patient. He averred that the American Government and MacArthur were neither consulting nor informing the Soviet Government about what was happening in Japan. Thus, it could not bear responsibility for MacArthur's actions. Therefore, the Soviet representative in Japan, General Kuzma Derevyanko, was being recalled. The Soviet Government, he almost declaimed, had self-respect as a sovereign state. It was being treated not as an ally but as an American satellite in the Pacific; that role it would not accept, either in the Far East or anywhere.

Harriman was genuinely puzzled. He said there must be a complete misunderstanding. The President, he asserted, had certainly not intended to disregard the views of the Soviet Government or keep it uninformed. In the first days of the occupation, he knew, the Supreme Commander had sent ample information to the Soviet General Staff through the American Military Mission in Moscow. What had happened subsequently? To his knowledge it had been arranged that General Derevyanko should be able to communicate with Russia by radio, and he had assumed that he was keeping the Soviet General Staff and Stalin informed. Stalin's complaints surprised him and he would report them to Washington. But the Marshal was not done; if this regime were to continue, he repeated, the Soviet Union would leave Japan. It would be more honest to do so than to remain "as a piece of furniture."

As the discussion went back over the same ground, Stalin warmed up to his theme; the formation of the Advisory Commission was not the right solution; if he sent a representative to it he feared that would interfere with its work and hurt Soviet-American relations. So, he asked—perhaps himself rather than Harriman—would it not be wiser to step aside and let the Americans do what they wanted in Japan? The Soviet

Government would not interfere. Perhaps from now on it would adopt a policy of isolation, the policy which had so long been favored by the United States. Perhaps there was nothing wrong with that course.

Harriman answered with spirit, remarking that in the Control Councils for Rumania and Bulgaria the American and British members had been so badly treated that they were upset in the same way as Stalin now seemed to be. The Marshal broadened the area of reciprocal accusation; in the Balkans, he rejoined, the Americans had been treated as well as the Russians had been in Italy, and in fact were now being treated better. Moreover, should not the Russian part in the Japanese war be taken into account? The Russians had maintained more than twenty divisions on the Manchurian front for ten years and at the end had brought seventy divisions into action against Japan. Beyond that they had been ready to assist the United States by landing troops in the Japanese islands but the American Government had rejected the offer.[2]

Stalin's tone may have been due in part to a brusque encounter between MacArthur and Derevyanko. As retold by the Supreme Commander—perhaps enlivened by his customary dramatic flourish—Derevyanko had maintained that Soviet troops in Japan would have to be entirely independent of MacArthur's authority. "I refused point blank. General Derevyanko became almost abusive and threatened the Soviet Union would see to it that I was dismissed as Supreme Commander. He went so far as to say Russian forces would move in whether I approved or not. I told him that if a single Soviet soldier entered Japan without my authority, I would at once throw the entire Russian mission, including himself, in jail. He listened and stared as though he could not believe his

[2] Edward Page, the Foreign Service officer who acted as translator and wrote the memos of these talks, added a note, something which he seldom did. "When Stalin made this remark it was quite obvious from the tone of his voice and the expression on his face that he was still very irked at our refusal to permit Soviet troops to land in Hokkaido."

ears, and then said politely enough, 'By God, I believe you would.' He turned and left, and I heard nothing more of it." [3]

Harriman knew nothing of this encounter. But perceiving no use in continuing the argument, he merely remarked that his information differed from Stalin's. Moreover, this was past history. In a regretful tone, he summed up the immediate result of their talk; Stalin would not consent to send a representative to the meeting of the Advisory Commission, wanting to discuss the Soviet proposal for a Control Council directly with the American Government since he thought the Commission could not decide it. Stalin confirmed this summary. Thereupon Harriman said he would report on their conversation fully to Washington.

In doing so, he told Byrnes that "In spite of a number of blunt remarks, Stalin had never discussed matters in a more calm and open manner. . . . It is my feeling that he wants to work things out with us but he is inordinately suspicious of our every move [and] that we are trying to put something over on him." Harriman said he thought Stalin was fearful that if he sent a representative to the meeting of the Advisory Commission, and presented there the proposal for an Allied Council, there would be open disagreement—as there had been in London. He wanted to know first what we were going to do about the Council.

Harriman remarked that he had no information about how General Derevyanko was treated in Tokyo. But it seemed to him advisable to keep Stalin constantly informed of our intentions and of what we were trying to accomplish in Japan. For, he added, the way in which the situation had gone, Stalin now thought suspiciously that we might intend to disregard the Soviet Union in the conduct of Japanese affairs; and this could lead to great difficulties in other directions. Harriman thought that if a way could be found to satisfy Stalin about the arrangements for the control of Japan, the existing differ-

[3] Douglas MacArthur, *Reminiscences*, New York, McGraw-Hill Book Company, 1964, p. 285.

ences about procedure for the making of the European peace treaties—which had been reduced as the result of his talks with Stalin—could be bridged.

Their conversation had brought no conclusive change of mind, nor any immediate adjustment in the tactics or terms of either government. Yet it was a clarifying preface to the negotiations that followed, which—as we shall see—did produce at least the semblance of accord.

VII

The Wearisome Interim Negotiations

Byrnes, in his memoirs, avers that Stalin's insistence on knowing the American view on the control of Japan ". . . was a revelation." [1] When Molotov had raised the question of Japan in London, Byrnes had thought it to be simply part of his war of nerves. Now, Byrnes related, "we suddenly realized that we had been wrong."

While this may explain Byrnes' surprise, his memory failed when he also wrote in the memoirs, "Mr. Harriman was as surprised as he was unprepared. . . ." The Ambassador had repeatedly forewarned Byrnes that Stalin would want to discuss the subject and had requested instruction as to what he should tell Stalin. In any case, the quest for an arrangement that might be acceptable to Moscow was now pursued with zeal, if not with zest.

Washington began to study more alertly the thoughts and actions of the Soviet authorities about Far Eastern situations.

During the last week in October the Soviet press continued to allege that the new Japanese Cabinet, headed by Shidehara, whose entry into office MacArthur had arranged or

[1] James F. Byrnes, *Speaking Frankly*, New York, Harper & Brothers, 1947, p. 108.

approved, was reactionary; that it was trying to evade the fulfillment of the terms of surrender and the punishment of war criminals and was refusing to take measures necessary to democratize Japanese political life. *Pravda* predicted that the appointed cabinet would defend the reactionary constitution which in the past had legalized the combination of monopolies and military cliques.

On October 27 Byrnes told Harriman of a new proposal which, however, had not yet been cleared with MacArthur.

The American Government would agree that there should be an Allied Military Council as well as an Advisory Commission. This was to be made up of the Supreme Commander (chairman) and representatives of the Soviet Union, China, and the British Commonwealth. The Supreme Commander would be the sole executive authority for the Allies within the area of his command and would issue all orders for the *implementation* of supplementary directives and of the surrender terms and the occupation of Japan. He was to be obligated to ". . . consult and advise with the Council upon orders involving questions of principle in advance of their issuance, the exigencies of the situation permitting." But his decision was to be controlling.

MacArthur consented with misgivings to put up with the presence of the Allied Military Council only because he was assured that he would not be subordinate to it or dependent upon its assent. Thus, two days later, on October 29, Byrnes, on advising Harriman that he was informing the Chinese and British Governments of this new proposal and that the Ambassador might proceed to tell Molotov of it, said that he hoped this arrangement would serve, since it would be extremely difficult if not impossible for the American Government to modify it in any important particular.

Without waiting for the Soviet response to this proposal, the American Government decided to go ahead with the scheduled meeting of the Far Eastern Advisory Commission.

However, as Byrnes also told Harriman, it was contemplated that this first meeting would be short and ceremonial; it would name the American member temporary chairman, and then adjourn for a week to allow all governments to consider the revised terms of reference which should strengthen and expand its authority somewhat.

Since in the message of October 29 the Secretary of State said that the Ambassador could, if he thought it advisable, see Stalin again after talking with Molotov, Harriman rushed back several queries about points that he thought Stalin would raise. He reminded Byrnes that the Marshal had indicated that he would agree to some such terms for an Allied Council as the American Government now proposed only on the assumption that the occupation forces would be solely American; and that he had stated that if forces of other nations formed part of the occupation army, the powers of the Supreme Commander would, of necessity, have to be restricted. So, Harriman asked, were other governments going to be invited to provide forces for the occupation? He was doubtful whether Stalin would agree to place any Soviet troops under MacArthur's command, since they might be ordered to carry out policies of which he did not approve. But, his conjecture continued, if the British and Chinese did put forces under MacArthur's command, Stalin might insist on the inclusion of Soviet forces also and a separate zone of occupation.

Harriman also expressed the opinion that Stalin would be likely to reject the proposed voting procedure in the Advisory Commission. According to this procedure a decision would require approval by a majority of the members, including three of the four principal powers; provided that pending action of the Commission on urgent matters, the American Government could issue any necessary interim directives to MacArthur. Harriman thought that Stalin would object to this reserved power, which would enable the American Government to present others with the choice of agreeing with it or having it act independently.

On November 1, after Molotov had had a chance to study the texts which Harriman had given him, he quizzed the Ambassador.

Where was the Military Council to meet? Harriman said in Tokyo.

Was the Military Council to be a control or an advisory body? Harriman said the control would be vested in the Supreme Commander, who would, however, consult with the other members of the Council.

What were to be the functions of the Council? Harriman said to consult with MacArthur on the *implementation* of the directives he received. If all members agreed, there would be no problem; if there was a difference of opinion, MacArthur would decide. All directives would be issued in the name of the Supreme Commander, not in the name of the Council. Molotov chivvied away at this arrangement by citing the textual changes that had been made in the provisions under which the Control Council of Hungary acted. These, he alleged—paying homage to language rather than actuality—stipulated that policy directives would be issued only *after* agreement. Harriman reminded Molotov that Stalin at Sochi had agreed that the Supreme Commander in Japan should have the final say and that he was sure the American Government would not deviate from that requirement.

Would the occupation forces be all American? Harriman said that matter was still being discussed.

Could not the proposed voting procedure in the Far Eastern Advisory Commission be changed? Molotov's remarks indicated that the Soviet Government preferred to have the principle of unanimity of the four principal powers observed, and was disinclined to authorize the American Government to issue interim directives in case no agreement was reached. However, he said the Soviet Government was still considering the question.

This conversation on November 1 was the preface to a month of sharp and repetitive argument about the proposed rules for both the Advisory Commission and the Military Council. The issue in contention essentially was whether or not, or in what circumstances, the American Government and the Supreme Commander would have to secure Soviet assent to their policies and acts.

Diplomats had to endure patiently the seesawing ordeal of negotiations during this period. Historians—with their research assistants if they have them—may now study every turn and twist of every debated point every day in order to know and to judge what each of the advocates sought and the justifications they gave for their requests. But I, in this narrative, shall give only a greatly compressed account of them.

Molotov persistently sought to elevate the proposed Council in Tokyo into a group which would have the power to *control* the execution of the terms of surrender; or if that could not be achieved, to reduce MacArthur's right to take independent action. He advanced the proposal that if any other member of the Council differed with the Supreme Commander on questions of principle, he was to postpone decision until the governments concerned reached an accord either directly or in the Advisory Commission. Harriman, with equal persistence, rebuffed this proposal, maintaining that the Supreme Commander must have controlling power, being merely under the obligation to consult with and seek advice of the Council. He denied, with ample reason, that the Control Council of Hungary was actually operating in the way which its revised statutes prescribed and Molotov described.

Molotov also sought various amendments to the provisions that were to govern the voting rules of the Advisory Commission. The chief of these was that decisions should require unanimous assent of all the four principal powers—as part of a majority.

Harriman, in reporting to Byrnes (on November 6), observed that Molotov was following his usual tactics of stepping up Soviet demands. It seemed to him clear that what Molotov asked might so hinder the American Government and the Supreme Commander that they would not be able to carry on the direction and occupation of Japan without Soviet approval. His surmise was that the Soviet Government was seeking to retain the chance to influence the *eventual* government of Japan and the steps by which it evolved. If, Harriman concluded, no solution was reached, the Russians might stay out of Japan and the disagreement might affect its action in other parts of the Far East and Europe. So he suggested that the American Government review its proposals once again in order to make its final position clear; and that once this had been done, he, as Truman's emissary, might again carry the questions at issue to Stalin.

Byrnes' appraisal of Molotov's proposals was the same as Harriman's. He thought they would produce the same difficulties as were being met in the control of Germany. He wanted the Soviet Government to realize that, on the one hand, no matter how it maneuvered, the American Government would not agree that either it or the Supreme Commander should be divested of or share the responsibility for making or enforcing final decisions. But that, correlatively, it wanted to do everything feasible to have its allies participate in the making of basic policies, and to advise and consult with them on the ways these policies were effectuated.

The forthright presentation of the American conception of the assignment and mode of operation of both the Allied Military Council and the FEAC, which Harriman made to Molotov on November 9, produced a stiffly argued response and induced a written statement of the Soviet appraisal of the American proposals. The Soviet Government accused the American Government of wanting to maintain without change all the rights and privileges which the Supreme Commander had enjoyed during the previous months, when at his discretion and without even informing Allied representatives he had established and changed the Japanese regime, and formed and dismissed the Japanese Government. Such a practice, in effect, would make any control group merely a façade, of which the Soviet Government would not want to be merely a figurehead.

It then averred that the American Government had not grasped Stalin's views accurately. Stalin, the statement continued, recognized that the United States had more responsibility in Japan than the other Allies, but he had never agreed that the United States alone should have this responsibility. Correlatively, Stalin recognized that the Supreme Commander, as chairman of the Control Council, should have decisive say on most questions; but he had not agreed that he should have it in regard to *all* questions. Decisions about matters of principle, such as a change in regime or in the composition of the Japanese Government, should not be made effective until and unless all the four principal Allies agreed upon them.

In the ensuing discussion with Harriman, Molotov developed this idea further; he averred that he was merely seeking to be assured that when *basic* questions, such as changes of the Japanese Government or constitution were under consideration, the other Allies—including the Soviet Union—would have to give their assent. Harriman met the point by asserting again that the American Government could not accept responsibility for the occupation without having the unqualified right to issue interim directives in the event of a disagreement between the members of the Council or the Advisory Commission.

This was the main span of difference between the American and Soviet positions. Harriman, in reporting to Washington on November 13, newly explained how the ideas of the Soviet officials now seemed to be tending. They believed that the other representatives on the Council would function only as advisors to the Supreme Commander and not have any real status or influence. He recalled that Stalin had said that he would not maintain a representative in Tokyo if he were to be merely a "piece of furniture"; Molotov had said that it would be unacceptable for the Soviet representative to be "merely decorative."

They were of the opinion, the Ambassador continued, that the decisions reached in the Advisory Commission would be only general, and would be vitally affected by the way in which they were carried out. Therefore the Soviet authorities were trying to have the name of the Council changed from Allied Military Council to Control Council. They were also insistent that this Council would have to be unanimous in its decisions on matters of principle when the question was not urgent. Otherwise the governments would be less likely to consult with each other adequately. The same desire, Harriman thought, explained the Soviet wish that the four principal powers should have the right of veto in the Advisory Commission on fundamental matters. Always mistrustful, the Russians were afraid that without such a rein on American policies Japan might be developed into a country that was antagonistic to the Soviet Union and a threat to it.

Harriman concluded his message by stating that he thought the situation was serious. Unless the Soviet Government was reasonably satisfied, it might decline to participate in the arrangements for Japan and might try to bolster Russian security in the Far East through other measures, which would be hostile to American policies and interests. Moreover, the Soviet attitude toward the United Nations and toward European situations would probably be affected. General F. N. Roberts, the American military attaché in Moscow, sent Marshall a message stating that he shared Harriman's conjecture about the consequence of failure to reach agreement with the Soviet Government.

Washington responded by trying anew to satisfy the Soviet Government without subjecting itself or the Supreme Commander to procedures that could indefinitely delay action and thus break down the American administration of control. Byrnes agreed on November 17 that it might be stipulated that the Allied Council (we were unwilling to have it named Allied "Control" Council but were willing to drop the word "Military" and have it named simply the Allied Council for Japan) should not change the regime of control for Japan or approve changes in the Japanese constitution unless authorized by the

Far Eastern Advisory Commission. Conformably he also said the American Government was willing to have it stipulated that this Commission should issue directives dealing with these matters only after consultation and agreement—*unanimous agreement* of the four principal powers. But it could not contemplate that the Supreme Commander might be unable to act when necessary in the event that agreement was not reached; for if he could not do so, his position would be weakened in dealing with the Japanese authorities and his task would become impossible. Therefore, Byrnes concluded, the provision authorizing the American Government to issue *interim* directives to the Supreme Commander must be retained. Any member who was dissatisfied with any order given by MacArthur or any action taken by him of a policy nature might ask the Advisory Commission to review it.

At the same time, Byrnes informed Harriman that the British Commonwealth had offered a balanced force of thirty thousand men. The American Government would accept and welcome a similar Soviet force. But, he said again, contingents of all countries would be integrated under MacArthur's command, and there would be no separate zones of occupation. When Harriman passed this information on to Molotov, the Soviet Commissar for Foreign Affairs recalled what Stalin had said about such an arrangement.

These amended proposals did not satisfy the Soviet Government. It protested particularly the drawstring on the rule of unanimity which would enable the American Government to overcome Soviet opposition even on matters which, in the current terminology, were called "matters of principle." These were 1) the provision in the terms of reference of the Advisory Commission which would allow the American Government to issue interim directives to the Supreme Commander in the event that agreement had not yet been reached; 2) the provision in the terms of the Council which would allow the Supreme Commander, if he thought it essential, to issue orders to implement his directives without waiting for the assent of the other members.

Tirelessly the Soviet Government continued to maintain that Soviet representatives in Hungary, Rumania, and Bulgaria were under restraints equivalent to those which it wished to impose upon the Americans in Japan. If the Soviet authorities thought they were being offered merely the thin end of partnership in Japan, the American officials who had been for months trying to get a chance to share in the control of these European countries knew that their requests and protests had been ineffectual, that the Soviet chairmen of the control organizations had ruled regardless.

At the end of November, with the two wills still in a tussle, Harriman summed up for Byrnes the several potentialities of the situation. Perhaps Stalin had really decided that unless Russia got an effective place in Japan it would remain aloof and free to retaliate; or perhaps he was keeping the situation in suspense pending the further course of negotiations about Eastern Europe.

Truman and Byrnes decided not to foreclose the issue— not to rush into new consultations with the Soviet Government.

Meanwhile the Far Eastern Advisory Commission proceeded cautiously with its assignment, leaving the way open for adaptation to changed circumstances or alterations of its constitution and procedure, and a place open for the Soviet Union.

The first meeting of the Commission, on October 30, had been only a ceremonial one. The Secretary of State had addressed it briefly. Then it had adjourned to allow the members to study more thoroughly the arrangements for its activities which the American Government was proposing. The bid for a Soviet member was still unrequited when the Commission next met on November 6, and came into more formal existence. The appointments of General Frank R. McCoy, the American member, as Chairman, and of Nelson T. Johnson, former Ambassador to China and Australia, as Secretary General of the Commission, were approved. Both individuals were thoughtful and experienced searchers and interpreters of the views of the associated governments.

During the continued wait for the Soviet Government to decide whether or not to accept membership, the Commission began actively to discuss the policies to be pursued toward and in Japan. An invitation to meet next in Tokyo—which the Supreme Commander had been inveigled into extending—was accepted.

MacArthur, for his part, was continuing to pursue with vigor and zest the execution of the many provisions of the terms of surrender. He was also, by this time, well started on the novel task of reforming and instructing the new Japanese Government which, with his approval, had come into existence.

VIII

If At First You Don't Succeed —

Harriman's report of his talks with Stalin and Molotov hitched the problem to those many others which had been left unsettled after the disputatious meeting in London. The difference over the procedure for making peace treaties remained. The ordinary methods of diplomacy were not quieting several other current situations: the continued and interfering presence of Soviet troops in Iran, the menacing Soviet claims against Turkey, and discord about what was to be done in Germany. Any one of these might lead toward an open break between the former allies. This would cause the first business meeting of the General Assembly of the United Nations, which was to be held in January, 1946, to be stricken with infantile paralysis. The American Government was hopeful that this new creation of nations would bring harmony. It planned to place before it a most important resolution for the international control of the new foe or friend of mankind—atomic energy.

Thus Byrnes acted incisively. He recalled that at Yalta it had been agreed that the Foreign Ministers of the three great powers—the United States, the Soviet Union, and Great Britain—should meet informally every three or four months. Might they not get the peace-making machinery in motion again? It was, Byrnes decided, worth a try. So a cable was sent to Molotov referring to the Yalta agreement, and pointing out that the three Foreign Ministers had met at San Francisco, Potsdam, and London, but not in Moscow. Byrnes suggested, therefore, that they get together in Moscow, very soon. He was sure that, Russian hospitality being what it was, the Soviet Government would extend the invitation, and believed that if the meeting was held in Moscow, where he would have a chance to talk to Stalin, we might remove the barriers to the peace treaties.[1] He may well have thought it might be easier to reach a satisfactory agreement about this issue if there were only three proponents. The American Government might be able to present the case for France, China, and the smaller Western Allies to the unsympathetic Russians better than they could themselves.

After consulting his colleagues, Molotov stated that he agreed that this meeting should take place, and in Moscow. But he suggested that it start a little later in order to leave sufficient time for preparation. It was agreed provisionally that the opening date might be set for December 15, so that Byrnes might get back to Washington by Christmas Eve.

Byrnes had informed Bevin at once of the message he sent to Molotov. The British Foreign Secretary and some of his Cabinet colleagues balked. They were doubtful whether the conference at that time would serve to bring the participants closer together rather than to separate them further. This skepticism marked the statement which the Lord Chancellor, Jowitt, made in the House of Lords on November 28, speaking for the Government. He said that he did not want to see a succession of meetings of Foreign Ministers which did not end in agreement, and established the habit of disagreement. "My own view," he said, "is that many of these international conferences depend upon the spade work which was done beforehand, and I am sure that at the appropriate time, when it is considered that time has come, we should be very willing and

[1] Byrnes, *Speaking Frankly*, p. 109.

ready to resume at the point at which we left off."

In his reply to Byrnes, Bevin raised various objections. He believed that the effects of another failure to agree would be very serious and he did not think there was enough time left for the preparatory talks that would be necessary to insure success. He was afraid that if in this meeting, ideas of interest to China and France were discussed in the absence of these nations, they would be aggrieved. And lastly, he was of the opinion that the time had come to bring the matters that the Foreign Ministers were discussing into the broader forum of the United Nations.

But after further exchange of ideas about the subjects that were to be discussed, Bevin, though still hesitant, agreed to attend. On December 6, the day before the public announcement of the meeting, he was asked in the House of Commons whether a special effort should not be made to solve the differences between Britain and Russia. He boldly said, "I don't accept that they are drifting apart. Sometimes friendship grows stronger when they do not meet quite so often." He had no relish for mixing it up again with Molotov. And he had a suppressed sense of umbrage toward Byrnes because of the way in which the Secretary of State sometimes went ahead without consulting him, or even informing him in advance.

Identical public announcements about the Moscow Conference were made simultaneously in the three capitals. Care was taken not to arouse undue expectations. Yet diplomats discerned that the meeting might be of crucial importance. Coming after the quarrelsome meeting at London, it was thought that this second attempt would indicate, perhaps determine, whether the wartime allies would come closer again or split further away from one another. This would inevitably affect the prospects for the untested United Nations. And, since the world was still startled and frightened by the burst of the atom, this might decide whether this new and great form of energy could be confined, or whether the nations would strive in sinister rivalry to develop weapons having this awful destructive force. Was the fissured atom to be servant or tyrannical god?

The preliminary skirmishes between the three participating governments about the subjects to be discussed at Moscow indicated that the disagreement over the arrangements for Japan was going to be entangled with others.

In the list which it submitted, the American Government included not only Item 3, "The terms of reference of the Far Eastern Commission and the Allied Council for Japan," but also Item 5, "Disarming and evacuating the Japanese from North China," and Item 6, "Transfer of control of Manchuria to the Chinese National Government."

Circumstances led Byrnes to propose that these last two subjects be openly discussed. By December the American Government had become aware that the Chinese National Government might not be able to extend its authority over North China—where the Chinese Communists were lodged—unless given much greater help, at the risk of involving the United States in the Chinese civil war. Nor might the National Government be able to extend its authority over Manchuria, from which Soviet troops were being evacuated in such a way as to aid the Communist enemies of Chiang Kai-shek rather than his poorly equipped and poorly led armies.[2] The Ameri-

[2] General Albert Wedemeyer, Commander of U. S. forces in China and Chief of Staff to Chiang Kai-shek, in an important report (November 21) which he sent to the War Department, had defined the military alternatives succinctly. They were, he thought, either 1) to take all U. S. military personnel out of the China theater as soon as practicable, while continuing and increasing economic aid to the National Government, or 2) to announce our determination to continue to give military as well as economic support to the National Government until all Japanese forces were out of the Chinese theater of war and China had secured enough internal strength to take its "rightful" place among the nations. If that were done, he said, his orders would have to be changed so that in his

can Government had sent about fifty thousand marines into the main Chinese ports and airports to assist the Chinese Government to disarm the Japanese armies and arrange their return to Japan, and to help maintain order in the cities and railway connections. As one feature of its worried effort to devise a new and comprehensive plan of political and military unification for China, the American Government was planning to keep these divisions in China—despite the clamor for demobilization and the reluctance of the Joint Chiefs of Staff. General Marshall was going to China as the President's Special Representative, to try to induce the warring Chinese factions to enter into a coalition—to form a unified government and military force so that China could begin to reconstruct its life and society.

The American Government wished to avert Soviet resentment because it was going to keep our troops in China a while longer. It also wanted to retain if possible Russian cooperation in its efforts to unify China. And conjointly, while wishing Soviet armies out of Manchuria, it wanted the withdrawal to be so timed and so executed that the Chinese Government could take over the region and the Communists could be kept out. This was a formidable assignment for

direction of U. S. and Chinese forces he need no longer be careful not to get involved in the Chinese civil war.

Wedemeyer recommended that Chiang Kai-shek devote his resources to controlling the situation in Central China, since he would not be able to stabilize the situation in North China for months, perhaps years, without reaching an accord with the Chinese Communists, and would not be able to recover Manchuria for many years unless the National Government reached a satisfactory accord with both Chinese Communists and the Soviet Government. He believed the chances of an accord with the Chinese Communists "remote."

In view of the deficiencies of Chiang Kai-shek's civilian government and armies, he recommended that Manchuria be placed at once under a joint trusteeship of the United States, Great Britain, and the Soviet Union.

The American Government was trying to avoid these dilemmas and these risks by sponsoring the effort at unification of China.

Marshall in China, a hard and slippery one for Byrnes in Moscow.

As soon as Molotov looked over the American list, he asked Harriman to explain the item which concerned the disarmament and evacuation of Japanese armed forces in North China. He also suggested that the conference might concurrently consider the evacuation of American forces from China and the withdrawal of British forces from Greece.

Byrnes, on December 9–10, told Harriman that the reason for suggesting that the question of evacuation of Japanese forces from North China be discussed was that there were still 300,000 Japanese in the region who had not yet been disarmed and evacuated because of the civil strife going on there. He simply wanted to explain the situation to Molotov (and Bevin), and to present the reasons why American troops were being kept there. He said that it would be hard to reach a conclusive understanding about the presence and actions of American forces in China because the Chinese Government would not have a representative at Moscow.

But—taking cognizance of the junctions made by Molotov—Byrnes said he would be glad of the chance to exchange views informally on the withdrawal of Allied troops from *all independent states* other than Japan and Germany. To what countries did Byrnes refer, Harriman inquired at once. He was not provided with a precise definition. As it turned out, he did not need one. For even without knowing just what countries Byrnes had in mind, both Bevin and Molotov demurred. They did not want to spread the net of discussion from China to the whole occupied world. Bevin said that he saw no reason to discuss the withdrawal of British troops from Greece. Molotov informed Byrnes that he thought discussion of the withdrawal of Allied forces from all independent states would be *inexpedient*, especially since Soviet troops were in the territory of other countries on the basis of either armistice of other special agreements in force.

Thus Byrnes was left with the problem of reaching an agreement about the control of Japan, and stilling Soviet protests over the continued sojourn of American forces in China, without affecting Russian actions in Manchuria. The course of the conference was to show that the Soviet Government was not entirely unwilling to go along with the wishes of the American Government in these regards once the United States relaxed its resistance to Soviet domination of the countries of Southeastern Europe. The Soviet Government would go after the bird in hand and wait and watch before chasing the two birds that might be in the bush.

IX

Moscow —
The Correlated Negotiations

Byrnes got to Moscow after a hazardous and tense flight through a heavy snowstorm. At one point the pilot, flying low in search of identifying objects, asked permission to look around for a few minutes, and to take the diplomatic explorers back to Berlin if need be, which the gas supply then remaining would permit. Byrnes said that he might keep on trying to find his way, but that Napoleon and Hitler had failed to reach Moscow and he, too, would not oppose a retreat. But they were brought down safely. Apropos of this historical analogy, a comment in the December 17 Chicago *Tribune* may have amused its coterie of readers, if not the delegation. "Byrnes arrived in Moscow in mid-December wearing a light topcoat. This throws a good deal of light on (A) his intellectual preparation for his job or (B) the qualities of foresight that our best diplomats possess. For Napoleon and Hitler it may be said that they both expected to get to their goal before cold weather set in. They, at least, had heard about it."

Byrnes and his associates needed not only intellectual preparation but stamina. For the national delegations set right to work and kept working up to almost the hour of departure

—morning, noon, and night. The unrelenting schedule left no leisure time, not much time for deliberation, and too little time for sleep. Byrnes conveys to professionals the rigor of the schedule when in his memoirs he comments, "I doubt if anyone else has spent even a fraction of the time I did in Moscow and has seen so little of the city. Besides Spasso House [the American Embassy], where we worked and managed to get a few hours of sleep each night; Spridinovka House, where the council held its sessions; and the Kremlin, where we had our meetings with Stalin, the only other thing I saw in Moscow was the Opera House where the Foreign Ministers were entertained by the Soviet Government." [1] Diplomats at summit conferences—or near-summit conferences—are the slaves of their problems; they have not the respites and relaxation of business executives, bankers, professional men, or salesmen meeting in convention. Time has them by the ear.

Having, I hope, given enough indication of the variety and complexity of the matters that were to be discussed in Moscow, I will leave students of that concourse to tell adequately of each and all of them. This narrative will touch only on such subjects of negotiation as were, either explicitly or implicitly, closely related to the contest over the control of Japan.

Around the conference table various plays of wit and will went on at the same time, the negotiators being both authors and actors, often changing their lines in an unfinished script. A movie camera and recorder might convey the conjunction; historical narration can only etch them uncertainly, for documents are often opaque and memories flickering and self-regarding. And so many of the records are still interred in the archives.

Both Byrnes and Bevin called on Molotov on December 15 before the formal meetings began. Harriman urged Byrnes

[1] *Speaking Frankly*, p. 111.

to use this chance to clear up with Molotov the precise meaning of some of the ropy points in the Soviet proposals about the arrangements for the control of Japan and various other matters. Thereby he could learn, perhaps, whether the chance for compromise was good or poor, and how it might be reached without protracted formal argument. Byrnes seemed to agree that this was a good idea. But his short first talk with Molotov was consumed in identifying the subjects that were to be discussed. Bevin's conversation was spent similarly "in arranging" as bridge-players say as they sort out their cards.

Soon after the courtesy speeches had been made at the first meeting on the sixteenth, Molotov went on the offensive. He asked that the question of atomic energy be placed last, not first, on their order paper. Byrnes attributed this Soviet proposal to lack of interest. Perhaps so in one sense, not in another. Almost certainly the Soviet Government was at the time evaluating the chance and cost of emulating us in the nuclear field, and also wanted further to test the world political balance. But a definitive explanation could come only from Soviet sources, and is hardly to be expected soon. Byrnes had already agreed to this shift, and on so learning, Bevin said he would not object. Thus any possibility that the wrangle over smaller issues of national importance would be quieted by common interest in this far greater and more enduring issue, passed.

Then Molotov made his next play. He asked that two subjects not yet certified for discussion should be included: the withdrawal of American troops from China and of British troops from Greece. Byrnes, he remarked, had been dodging discussion of the first question, Bevin dodging discussion of the second. Byrnes spoke up at once; the American Government was willing to explain and discuss the question of troop withdrawal from China, but it could not reach a conclusive understanding at this conference since no representative of China was here and the government must be consulted. Moreover, he wanted also to discuss—concurrently if not conjunctively—the withdrawal of Allied troops from all independent countries (Japan and Germany were occupied, not truly independent). Molotov broadened the area of tactical negotiation; he thought the situation in Indonesia (still a colony) should also be discussed. And the Soviet Government saw no need to talk over the question of transfer of control of Manchuria to the Chinese National Government—since the Soviet and Chinese Governments had a special agreement concerning Manchuria, over which they were not quarreling.

Bevin, in his reply, said it would be premature to discuss the withdrawal of British troops from Greece until they determined whether and how progress was being made toward the peace treaties. As regards Indonesia, he argued that the British forces in that country were acting under orders of those who had signed the surrender terms with Japan, including the Soviet Union; that the British Government was only the agent of the Supreme Commander in Southeast Asia (Admiral Lord Louis Mountbatten). He did not want "to be put on the carpet" in the present situation. Byrnes said that he hoped that Bevin would be willing to talk it over informally. Bevin said, in substance, "All right, but I think the talk would be more likely to incite argument than to create agreement."

Then Byrnes, the adjuster, remarked that if Molotov's proposal that Indonesia be listed on the agenda was a reflex response to the American proposal that the transfer of authority in Manchuria be discussed, he would withdraw that proposal, since his purpose had been to get information rather than review the actions of the Soviet Command. Whether or not the Secretary of State also thought thereby to divert Soviet objections to the continued presence of American troops in China, no memo or memoir tells. But so habitual and quick was Byrnes' impromptu adaptation of tactics, his tongue did not have to explain his reasons to his brain. Molotov was not downed. What he had in mind, he said, was not the execution of the armistice terms, but the rebellion in Indonesia and the intervention of the British troops. Why should that not be discussed informally in view of the proposals to discuss the questions of China and Iran? But as regards Manchuria, he repeated, he saw no need for discussion since the Soviet troops were staying in Manchuria only by request of the Chinese Government. This moving chain of argument was braked by an agreement that all of these situations in which Allied troops were in some other country—for short or long, for honest or disguised purposes—would be omitted from the agenda and left on the margin of the Conference. Had they not been, the discussions would have flared out, interminably. And probably no accord about the arrangements for the control of Japan could have been extricated from them.

The first item on the agenda, as finally agreed, was the resumption of discussion on procedure for settling terms of the peace treaties. The second was the terms of reference of the Allied Council for Japan and the Far Eastern Advisory Commission.

This first session of the conference left its mark on the impressions and expectations of all three participants. Byrnes remained resolved that Soviet-American relations should not become grooved in opposition. But he was compelled to recognize that Molotov was to be exigent and stubborn down to the last pinch. The Soviet Commissar was by nature, training, and habit mistrustful; he may have suspected that the reason Byrnes and Bevin were favoring informal discussions on so many subjects of interest might be a wish to be able to slip out later from any commitment. Bevin was uneasy and glum. He was sure that the Soviet Government was trying to weaken the British position in the whole Middle East, as shown by its thrusts against Greece and Turkey, and in Iran, and by its demand to be designated as trustee for one of the former Italian colonies in the eastern Mediterranean. He remarked to Byrnes that just as a British admiral, on seeing an island, always wanted to grab it, so the Soviet Government, on seeing an exposed land area, wanted to acquire it. The Soviet Government, it seemed to him, was seeking to form an area which it would dominate from the Balkans to the Adriatic in the west and Port Arthur or beyond in the east. The United States had their "Monroe sphere on the American continent and were extending it into the Pacific." Where would that leave the British and other European empires? Was the world to be divided into three "Monroe areas?" Byrnes tried to correct Bevin's view of American aspirations; we did not seek empire in the Pacific nor intend to try to control the life of Pacific countries; all we wanted were scattered bases and islands that had but few inhabitants, for our protection.

Byrnes had circulated copies of three memos setting forth in full the amended proposals for the control of Japan to which the American Government at this time sought approval. The changes made in cognizance of objections to the former ones were pointed out. To three in particular significance was attributed.

The Commission was renamed, the qualifying adjective—"Advisory"—being dropped; it would be called the Far Eastern Commission.

As first conceived, it was to have been authorized only to make recommendations to the governments concerned; but in this amended conception it was accorded authority to determine policies, principles, and standards for carrying out the terms of surrender and the occupation. However, the concurrence of all four major Allies was required for decision.

Additionally, the American Government agreed to the formation of a four-power Allied Council in Tokyo. This was to bring together the Supreme Commander, as American member and chairman, and Soviet, Chinese, and British Commonwealth members to consult with and advise him in regard to carrying out the terms of surrender, the occupation and control of Japan, and supplementary directives. The expanded scope of its interest was marked by the omission of the word

"Military" in its designation.

Bevin said that in general the revised American proposals were acceptable. Privately he asked Byrnes if Australia could not be given a place on the Allied Council—as fifth member. Byrnes said he was afraid not, since if it was, other countries would also claim a place. Bevin also reminded Byrnes of the standing request that India be represented on the Advisory Commission; Byrnes said he would insist on this even though the Soviet Government continued to object.

As Harriman definitely expected, and Byrnes should have anticipated, the Soviet authorities were still not satisfied. All their criticisms were heard again and at tedious length—in subsequent sessions (on December 18, 19, and 20). Molotov, after some placatory remarks, proposed the same amendments that he had been pressing in previous talks.

As regards the Council which was to meet in Tokyo: 1) It was to be named the Allied Control Council. 2) Its assignment was to be defined as being "for the purpose of *control over* the execution of the terms of surrender." 3) The obligation of the Supreme Commander to consult the Council on questions of principle was not to be qualified as it was in the American proposal by the clause "*the exigencies of the situation permitting.*" 4) In regard to matters of principle, including a change in the Japanese Government as a whole (i.e., not merely of individual members) decisions of the Supreme Commander were not to be put in effect before agreement (*soglasvanie*) in the Far Eastern Commission.

As regards the Far Eastern Commission: 1) The American Government should not be authorized to issue directives to the Supreme Commander about fundamental matters such as changes in the Japanese constitutional structure, or the regime of occupation, or of the government as a whole, except by prior agreement in the Commission—which would require the concurrence of all four major Allies. 2) And to prevent this veto power from being voided, the stipulation in the proposed terms of reference that "The American Government may issue interim directives to the Supreme Commander pending action by the Commission whenever urgent matters arise not covered by policies already formulated by the Commission" was to be omitted.

In essence, was the Soviet Union to have or not to have the right to hold up, perhaps nullify, decisions of the Supreme Commander, the American Government, and the Far Eastern Commission on vital matters and in crucial situations?

The mills of rationalization about these and related points ground on a week longer, producing much chaff but in the end enough alterations to make the garment of language fit both American and Soviet forms. But before examining these changes, we ought to note the turns in the correlated negotiations on other subjects. Particularly of interest are two series of conversations which went on concurrently with the final discussions about Japan—one related to Far Eastern situations, and the other concerned with the European peace treaties and the governments of Southeastern Europe. For the settlements reached on all of these were, I believe, connected with one another in a flickering but discernible balancing of advantage.

X

Moscow —
The Correlated Negotiations *Continued*

Molotov, when talking with Harriman, professed to be puzzled by the American proposal that the Moscow Conference discuss the disarming and evacuation of Japanese forces from North China. He may have inferred that our real purpose was to try to make sure that the Soviet Government would not uphold the demand of the Chinese Communists that the Japanese troops in that area should surrender to them—in defiance of General Order No. 1.

Byrnes issued an explanatory statement. The American Marines were in North China, he said, only to assist the Chinese Government to demobilize and deport the Japanese troops in the area, and ". . . will be withdrawn when they are no longer required for the purpose stated. We hope that will be soon."

Through the American mission headed by General Marshall which was beginning its operations in China, we were trying to bring together the various political elements and concurrently to arrange for a truce between opposing military forces in North China. If we were successful, "That would facilitate and speed the demobilization and deportation of

Japanese troops from China and hasten the day—which we sincerely hope to be soon—when the American Marines will be returned to the United States." Byrnes was heeding the admonition of the Joint Chiefs of Staff not to get the shrinking American forces involved in a land war in Asia.

Molotov's first response (on December 19) was ambiguous. Probably with an inner smirk he explained the slow withdrawal of Soviet troops from Manchuria as a favor granted to Chiang Kai-shek to enable him to get his own troops into Mukden, in Manchuria. The Generalissimo, he remarked, was exaggerating the number of opposing Chinese Communist forces in Manchuria and North China in order to get others to do the job for him there. The Secretary of State merely repeated his explanations. He refrained from mentioning the verified reports that Soviet military commanders in Manchuria were timing the departure of their troops in different localities so that the Chinese Communists might take over as soon as the Soviet troops were on the march. Soviet commanders, in face of the protests of Chinese Communist commanders, were also refusing to enable American naval transports to land Chinese Government troops at Dairen and other Manchurian ports from which they could most expeditiously move north.

Soon after this talk, Molotov circulated a memo which signaled a swerve in Soviet tactics. In this the Soviet Government noted that in the statement about American policy which President Truman had issued on the occasion of Marshall's departure for China (December 16) he had said that American armed forces, brought to China to disarm the Japanese, would stay there to bring about the stabilization of the internal situation in China. At this time, Molotov said, it is "known" that Japanese troops in North China were being drawn into military operations on the Government side. The interference of foreign troops in the internal affairs of China, the Soviet Government could not but believe, would aggravate the civil political struggle. In contrast, Soviet troops were being kept in

Manchuria one month longer only at the request of the Chinese Government. Thus the Soviet Government thought "it would be right" for it and the American Government to arrive at an understanding to evacuate their forces from China (including Manchuria) simultaneously, and not later than the middle of January, 1946.

Byrnes said the American Government took a different view of the situation. The United States was supporting the Chinese Nationalists—and so was the Soviet Union. This was a reference to the promise given in the Sino-Soviet agreement which had been signed in August, of which the Soviet Government was now being forgetful. Therefore, Byrnes said, with passive expression, it would not be in accord with "common policy" to do anything that would put the Nationalists in a more difficult position. He hoped the Soviet Government would cooperate in its efforts to foster political unification of all of China. Molotov—having made his point—said the Soviet aim was identical and did not argue further.

Probably he knew that Stalin, who was to talk with Byrnes that same evening (December 23), was going to be more detached or dissimulating. For so he turned out to be. After Byrnes had repeated his explanations and avowals, which terminated in the statement that the United States would like to take its troops out of China the very next day but circumstances and obligations made that difficult, Stalin said the Soviet Government would have no objection if the United States wished to leave its troops in China, but would merely like to be told about it. He went on to remark that he thought the Chinese Government greatly exaggerated the size of Chinese Communist forces, that fifty thousand Chinese Government troops ought to be enough to disarm the Japanese troops in North China. When Byrnes then remarked that Mao Tsetung claimed to have 600,000 troops in the Tientsin area, Stalin laughed heartily and said for the second time that "all Chinese were great boasters."

Thus the anxiety about adverse reactions of the Soviet

Government to the continued sojourn of American Marines in North China and to the Marshall Mission was quieted. This may have caused Byrnes to be a little more disposed to accommodate Soviet wishes in regard to the arrangements for the control of Japan—as far as might be done without risking critical interference with our purposes or interests.

The accord about Korea that was reached almost simultaneously may have also increased the disposition to seek a compromise about the arrangements for the exercise of control over Japan. It had been agreed at Potsdam that Korea should be placed under a joint trusteeship of the Soviet Union, the United States, Great Britain, and China. But no steps had been taken to create it, and the Korean political leaders were unenthusiastic about it. North of the 38th parallel Soviet forces were in control and were beginning to foster a Communist administration. South of that parallel American troops were in control and were finding that efforts to improve living conditions were being frustrated by division between the zones, and that discontent was spreading.

Reports of pending trouble had caused Byrnes weeks before this Conference at Moscow to inform Molotov that the American Government would like to explore the chances of reaching a working agreement with the Soviet Government that would enable trade, transport, and people to move freely between zones, and would inaugurate uniform or unified fiscal policies for the whole of Korea. But the Soviet Government had refused to authorize the Commanding General in the North to negotiate with the American General, Courtney H. Hodges, in the South about these and related subjects. Byrnes, after recalling this abortive effort, brought the subject up in the Conference. He outlined a somewhat more complete conception of unified administration—as preliminary to four-power trusteeship. Molotov professed to be taken aback by the breadth of the proposal, and asked for time to consult colleagues and advisers who knew more about the situation in

Korea. Byrnes proceeded at a later session (December 17) to present in a systematic form his proposal: that the four powers should begin discussions of a unified Korean administration under a joint trusteeship—acting in behalf of the U.N. and the people of Korea—which would bring an independent Korean government into existence within five years.[1]

Molotov responded with a proposal that seemed to conform to American conceptions of aims and procedures. It contemplated 1) the creation of a provisional democratic government which was to take the needed measures to develop industry, transport, and agriculture in *all* of Korea; 2) instruction to the Soviet and American military commands in Korea to form a *joint commission* to help form this provisional Korean Government and to formulate and recommend the necessary measures—in consultation with Korean democratic parties and social organizations; 3) almost immediate discussions between the commanders to work out measures for coordinating the two commands in economic and administrative matters.

Byrnes had only one amendment of consequence to put forward: that the British and Chinese Governments also be given a chance to consider the recommendations of the joint commission. To this Molotov readily agreed. Bevin was satisfied.

Thus three governments appeared to be nearing accord

[1] The Commanding General of the U.S. forces in Korea, General Hodges, was urging action; his messages to the War Department reported that the division of Korea was making it impossible to form a sound economy, that resentment against the American occupation forces was rising, that the Russians were fortifying North Korea and recruiting and arming North Koreans. He stressed his opinion that "The situation demands positive action as nothing could be worse than to allow it to drift to an ultimate crisis." The actions he advocated were unification, abandonment of the idea of trusteeship, confirmation of the promise of independence, and complete separation between Korea and Japan in the minds of the American officials, press, public, and the Allied Governments. The Joint Chiefs of Staff and Secretary of War concurred in this urgent plea for vigorous action.

about the aims and policies to be pursued in Korea and the procedures for effectuating them. Only persons soaked in mistrust could have resisted the cheerful conclusion that the Soviet Government was going to abstain from using its advantageous position in Korea to thwart us in Japan or China. Though American officials may have been unsure whether the Soviet Government would really permit Korea to be unified under an independent regime, they did not foresee that the Soviet Government was going to disregard the agreement completely.

At a far greater distance from Japan geographically than Korea, but I believe, more closely conjoined in Stalin's mind, was the still active contest about the future of Southeastern Europe. Stalin and Molotov were maintaining Soviet claims of primacy, for reasons akin to those adduced by the American Government vis-à-vis Japan. There the Soviet armies were in occupation just as the American soldiers were in Japan, with the American fleet offshore. So, all that Byrnes and Bevin could purchase with their diplomatic coin were packets of promises, the value of which they knew depended on Russian intentions and good faith. Stalin kept the store and held the scales.

It had been virtually settled that there would be three stages in the production of the peace treaties with Italy, Rumania, Bulgaria, Hungary, and Finland.

The first would be the drafting of the preliminary terms of peace. The American and British Governments had acceded to Soviet stipulation that this would be done in each case only by those governments which had signed the armistice terms against that particular enemy; the 4-3-2 formula, it was called—4 standing for the nations (including France) concerned with the treaty with Italy; 3 for the nations which would draft the treaties with Rumania, Bulgaria, and Hungary; and 2 for the Soviet Union and Great Britain, the two which alone would prepare the preliminary text of the treaty with

Finland. The resultant provisional texts were then to be submitted to a peace conference or peace conferences. There, other participants in the war would have a chance to comment and present their claims and recommendations. The third and conclusive stage would be the drawing up and signature of final texts of the treaties.

At Moscow the negotiations centered mainly about the second stage—the general peace conference or conferences. How inclusive or exclusive should be the group of countries invited to be present? Molotov, at first, would have had it ruled that only those countries that had actively waged war against each particular former enemy should be admitted; under this rule only five countries would have been qualified to consider the Bulgarian and Hungarian treaties respectively —the three great powers, Yugoslavia, and Greece for the Bulgarian treaty, Czechoslovakia replacing Greece for the Hungarian treaty; only the big-three powers would have qualified to consider the Rumanian treaty; and the Soviet Government alone would have been concerned with the treaty with Finland. In effect, Molotov's proposal visualized not one peace conference but five rather separate ones.

Byrnes stood up, as before, for inclusiveness. He presented a list of countries that ought to be enabled to consider all five of the peace treaties. This included *all* members of the United Nations that had actively waged war against the European members of the Axis. Bevin agreed with Byrnes. Molotov rested his argument on Soviet interpretation of certain articles in the agreements at Yalta and Potsdam. Byrnes and Bevin rested theirs on the opinion that the war against the Axis had been just one war. Strategy had been global; as partner in a common cause against the enemy combination, each of the Allies had served where it could best; where, and against which particular enemy, had been determined by geography and the exigencies of strategy and tactics. Moreover, Byrnes argued that the chance to participate in the peace conference was minimum recognition of the contribution of smaller Allies to the war, since the greater powers were retaining the right to be the ultimate judges and determinants of the terms of peace. Molotov contended that if the peace conference was to be thrown open to all of those Allies sponsored by the American and British Governments, places must also be found for two component states of the Soviet Union—White Russia and the Ukraine—and for the representatives of what he denominated as the three Baltic republics.

Lists were rewritten, shortened and lengthened. Entries were balanced against each other on scales that had two different dials; one registered the contribution to victory, the other registered the presumed political affiliation of each nominee. Were each move in this game of diplomatic adjustment to be recounted, readers would become as impatient as did the players.

When Byrnes and Bevin had separate interviews with Stalin on December 19, they both reviewed with him the whole range of the procedural argument. The Marshal accepted without comment the conception that there should be one general and inclusive conference. But he supported Molotov's contention that it would be advantageous and fair also to have present representatives of the two Soviet republics and of the three Baltic states. Certainly, he said, their contribution and suffering in the war against Hungary, Bulgaria, and Rumania gave them a better title to be present than Norway, Holland, and Belgium. When Byrnes said that if representatives of five Soviet republics and of five British dominions were accredited to the conference, the reasons would not be understood in the United States and the work of the conference would be prejudiced, the Marshal—without change of expression—went on to suggest that the representative of the United States at the conference might have six votes. Byrnes said that he would have to add five American states to the list—including his native South Carolina.

Bevin spoke up particularly in behalf of India, explaining how much it had done to assist in victory and the political usefulness of its presence.

These talks with Stalin stimulated the search for compromise about particulars. In ways, not explicitly acknowledged, the subsequent course of negotiations was calibrated—or should I say "intricated"?—with the negotiations on other issues over which differences remained between the Soviet Union and the Western Allies. Stalin in the end accepted the Byrnes list of states admissible to the peace conference.

The resultant accords were precise in detail. Provisions regarding the original drafting of the terms of the treaties and the determination of the final texts for signature deferred to the wishes of the Soviet Government. Provisions about the second—the conference—stage deferred to the wishes of the American and British Governments.

On the whole, the agreement was commendable. Had no accord been reached it is probable that the Western Allies would have proceeded on their own to conclude a peace treaty with Italy, and the Soviet Government would have proceeded on its own to conclude treaties with Hungary, Rumania, Bulgaria, and Finland. This divergence, concurrent with the emergent one over policies in Germany, would have split the war alliance more sharply and quickly. Moreover, had no agreement been reached about the procedure for arriving at the European peace treaties, the Conference at Moscow might have collapsed as had that at London—leaving the quarrel over Japanese affairs unabated.

Agreement was also reached about steps to reform the governments of Bulgaria and Rumania. Before the Moscow Conference the American and British Governments had recognized the provisional governments of Hungary and Austria on the understanding that free elections would soon be held. The Hungarians had voted on November 4 and the Austrians on November 25. In both countries the political parties with Communist affiliations were in a minority. The elected government in Hungary was mildly conservative; in Austria, mildly Socialist. The American and British Governments had promptly accorded them diplomatic recognition. American diplomats in Moscow and the Balkans were sure that the Soviet authorities were taken aback by the result, especially in Hungary; and that they became thereafter determined not to expose their position in Poland, Rumania, and Bulgaria to a similar test.

The American and British Governments had continued to deny recognition to the regimes in power in Rumania and Bulgaria. In October, Byrnes had sent a special representative to Rumania and Bulgaria—Mark Ethridge, editor of the Louisville *Journal*, of excellent repute, quick intelligence, and liberal tendencies. He had been instructed to ascertain whether the governments ". . . were broadly representative in the sense of the Yalta Declaration, which expressed the conviction of the Big Three that a lasting peace could be based only on fully representative and democratic governments, and whether the people of these governments would have an opportunity to vote in elections free from coercion and fear." [2]

In both countries Ethridge had talked with many persons of all elements of political and social opinion and interests. Soviet as well as local officials had been cooperative. Andrei Vishinsky, Deputy Commissar for Foreign Affairs, had talked over his observations with him.

Ethridge's report to Byrnes—sent to the Secretary on December 8 and circulated by him at the Conference at Moscow on December 18—was damning. One paragraph in his letter of transmittal conveys the gist of his conclusions:

> I must say in all honesty that both governments are authoritarian and dominated by one party, and that large democratic elements of the population in both

[2] The Yalta Declaration on Liberated Europe stipulated the three main Allies were "to concert during the temporary period of instability in liberated Europe [their] policies in assisting the peoples . . . to solve by democratic means their pressing political and economic problems."

Rumania and in Bulgaria have been forcibly excluded from representation in the government, while in Rumania particularly, former pro-Fascist collaborators and even some Iron Guardists occupy key positions.

The final paragraph expressed his hopeful indications of what the American Government might achieve by continued refusal to grant recognition until these regimes were reformed:

> While I fully concur with the need of the Red Army to protect its southern flank while it was actively engaged in Central Europe, the irritation which the Soviet Government may have felt in regard to the events of the past year in Greece and its concern over the question of the [Dardanelles] Straits, as well as the bitterness of the Russian people over the terrible ravage of the Rumanian army in the Ukraine, I feel that these considerations should now have much less weight and I trust that it will eventually be possible for the Russians and us to reach an agreement concerning these countries along the lines of those already reached with regard to the other former enemy countries in Eastern Europe [Austria and Hungary]. Particularly with regard to elections, I hope that the precedents of separate lists and civil liberties established in Austria and Hungary, agreed to by all three Yalta powers, may be applied in Bulgaria and Rumania.

The record of discussions at Moscow indicates that Ethridge missed two points of contact then outside of his purview. One was that the outcome of the elections in Austria and Hungary, which pained the Russians, was more likely to make them less rather than more willing to agree to genuine changes in the governments of Rumania and Bulgaria. The other was that the issues of control in these countries might be connected in Soviet reckoning with the disputed arrangements over the control of Japan and Greece. Yet they probably were connected; acceptance of the regimes in Bulgaria and Rumania, hidden behind a diplomatic formula, was the fee Stalin was determined to exact in equivalence to Soviet acceptance, also hidden behind formulas, of American dominance in Japan and British guardianship of the conservative government in Greece.

On December 18 Bevin had a far-reaching talk with Molotov. In spirited argument with the British Foreign Minister, Molotov used Greece as a justifying model for Soviet armed presence in the Balkans—as in arguments with Byrnes he used Japan. Mutual recriminations revealed how different were their versions of fact and interpretations of intention. Needless to remark, Molotov was his customary brazen self. He argued that the situation in Greece was completely different from those in Rumania, Bulgaria, and Hungary, since the Soviet armies were in the territories of these former enemies as a result of the armistice, while Greece had been an ally. He could see no military reason for the continued stay of British forces in Greece, while it was necessary for Soviet forces to remain in Rumania, Bulgaria, and Hungary to maintain the lines of communications with those in Germany. This was also the reason the Soviet forces were being kept in Poland. Finally, he contrasted the way in which British forces in Greece were intervening in the local political situation with the aloofness of Soviet armed forces, as shown by the way in which permitted elections in Hungary, Finland, and Bulgaria had gone. Neither, in short, gave ground.

When Byrnes handed Molotov, that same day, a copy of the Ethridge report, Molotov deprecated it, saying that of course Ethridge had known Byrnes' views and had been influenced by them. Byrnes followed up their talk by presenting the Conference with precise proposals for the reform of the Bulgarian and Rumanian governments which would make them representative and thus qualify them for recognition.

Molotov rejected the proposals and rebuffed the reasoning. So a few days later Byrnes carried the issue to Stalin. He said that he wished ". . . to talk about the Balkans 'as I have been having a difficult time with Mr. Molotov on this subject.' Stalin smiled broadly and said that this was unexpected news." [3] When Byrnes remarked that he thought if they could reach no agreement he would be compelled to publish the Ethridge report, Stalin gave a slight shrug and said if he did so he would ask Mr. (Ilya) Ehrenburg, the gifted Soviet publicist, "who was also an impartial man and had visited these countries," to publish his views.

Would not Stalin, Byrnes asked, suggest some plan to give genuine representation to parties not included in these governments? If that were done and followed by free elections, the United States could recognize them. Stalin answered by what he called a statement of basic facts: the Red Army was not exercising pressure on elections, as events in Hungary showed; all that the Soviet Union asked of the states that bordered or were near the Soviet Union was that they should be friendly —a natural wish since it had suffered much during the war from their actions—Hungarian troops had reached the Don and Rumanian troops had reached the Volga. As long as governments in power in these countries were "loyal," the Soviet Government did not wish to interfere in their internal affairs.

Still, Stalin agreed, though he was hesitant about it, perhaps the Bulgarian Government could be advised to include some members of the loyal opposition, though there could be no question of reorganization since elections had been held. In Rumania, Stalin said, where there had been no election, it might be possible to suggest to the Rumanian Government that it include representatives of the two large parties, but it would not be possible to suggest just what offices they were to be given. He assented to Byrnes' suggestion that a committee of three—Vishinsky and the American and British Ambassadors in Moscow (Harriman and Sir Archibald Clark-Kerr)—

[3] Byrnes, *Speaking Frankly*, p. 116.

be sent to Rumania to work out the plan for the inclusion of two additional members from parties outside the government. Stalin asked Byrnes to discuss this idea with Bevin; he did, and Bevin, though far from pleased, assented.

This cleared the way to an agreement—even as the way was being cleared on other subjects, including the arrangements for the control of Japan. But the ensuing argument over details, significant details, was arduous. Molotov, Byrnes, and Bevin wrangled over every turn of phraseology, every ounce of difference in the scale of reform. Through Christmas Day and into the last formal session of the Conference, on the twenty-sixth, the battle of wishes and wits went on. Byrnes and Bevin, in the end, concluded that the future of fostering independence in the Balkans and avoiding a dangerous struggle in the whole eastern Mediterranean and Middle East would be better served by assenting to a compromise that might leave Communist-oriented elements in control of Rumania and Bulgaria, than by merely refusing to recognize their governments. They could do so without feeling the cause was lost because they reserved the right of the American and British Governments, before granting recognition, to judge for themselves whether the delinquents had acted in good faith.

Moreover, there was the hope that after peace treaties were signed with Rumania and Bulgaria, Soviet troops would leave them, and that this would permit national elements, not subservient to Moscow, to recover control of their national life.

In the general atmosphere of renewed cooperation— coming after the rupture at London—it was more natural to trust than to mistrust, to hope rather than grimly conclude that the contest was unending. Byrnes and Bevin moreover were faced by the hard fact of geographical proximity, and there was the immovable Soviet army.

XI

Moscow—
The Accord About Japan

The contest over the control of Japan trickled to an end in the last two days of the Moscow Conference. Further small changes in the provisions about both the Council and the Commission emerged from the continuous turning of the wringer of negotiation.

On Christmas Eve, Stalin entertained the delegations at a banquet. There they were shown a Russian documentary movie. It portrayed the Russian attack in Manchuria. Impressive was the thoroughness of Russia's preparations for the Far Eastern war, indicative of the fact that Russia had been ready for a long and costly struggle—at the end of which its forces might have controlled all of Manchuria and the Korean peninsula and would probably have penetrated far into North China.

What, if any, thoughts Stalin had about the consequences of the unexpectedly abrupt end, is not to be known. But one of his toasts was an "atomic" toast.[1] Was he thinking of the lives of Soviet soldiers that had been saved? Or, with silent

[1] Associated Press dispatch from Moscow, *The New York Times*, December 26, 1945.

malice, of the futile attempt of the Americans to keep knowledge of the production of the weapon from him? Was he by his show of congratulation prolonging our ignorance of Soviet work on atomic fission, which had been going on? Or had he in mind the accord just reached to create a Commission under the United Nations to develop a plan for international control of atomic energy and its banishment from national arsenals? What the Americans thought the implications of the toast were, I don't know. Probably it was presumed to be just a jovial jest. All that is recalled is that everyone at the table lifted his glass in polite response.

The dinner marked the relaxation of argument. On the next day the last remaining serious difference was resolved by countervailing concessions. Molotov gave in to our insistence on retaining power to have our way if consultation did not bring assent. Byrnes accepted, however, limitations on the range of MacArthur's exercise of authority and the right of the American Government in the future to issue interim directives to him on matters of basic principle save with the acquiescence of the other major Allies. All existing directives —and these were comprehensive—were unaffected.

The essential features of the meshed provisions (almost as finely meshed as those in an insurance policy) may be most simply conveyed, I think, by summarizing them.[2]

FAR EASTERN COMMISSION

1) It was initially to have eleven members (including India).
2) Its main functions were:
   a) "To formulate the policies, principles and standards, in conformity with which the fulfillment by Japan of its obligations under the terms of Surrender may be accomplished."

[2] The full text of the sections of the Agreement on the Far Eastern Commission and Control Council as published in Sections II, III, and IV of the Joint Communiqué issued on December 27, is in Appendix 7.

b) "To review, on the request of any member, any directive issued to the Supreme Commander for the Allied Powers or any action taken by the Supreme Commander involving policy decisions within the jurisdiction of the Commission."

3) In doing so the Commission was to "proceed from the fact that there has been formed an Allied Council for Japan and will respect the existing control machinery in Japan, including the chain of command from the United States Government to the Supreme Commander and the Supreme Commander's command of occupation forces."

4) It could reach decisions by majority vote, provided that representatives of the United States, the United Kingdom, the Soviet Union, and China all concurred in the majority.

5) The American Government was to prepare directives in accordance with policy decisions of the Commission and transmit them to the Supreme Commander—who was charged with their implementation.

6) *Whenever urgent matters arose, the American Government was authorized to issue interim directives to the Supreme Commander pending action by the Commission.* However, this conclusive power was limited by a proviso that directives dealing with fundamental changes in the Japanese constitutional structure, or the regime of control, or with a change in the Japanese Government as a whole, would be issued only after the attainment of agreement in the Commission.

THE ALLIED COUNCIL

1) Its four members were to be the Supreme Commander (or his deputy), who was to be chairman and United States member, and representatives of the British Commonwealth, the Soviet Union, and China.

2) Its assignment was to consult with and advise the Supreme Commander in regard to the implementation of the terms of surrender, and the occupation and control of Japan.

3) The Supreme Commander was to issue all directives and be the sole executive authority for the Allied Powers.

4) The Supreme Commander was to consult and advise with the Council in advance of the issuance of orders on matters of substance, the *exigencies of the situation permitting*. His decision upon these matters was to be controlling.

5) However, should a member of the Council disagree with him on implementation of the Commission's policy decisions concerning a change in the regime of control, fundamental changes in the Japanese constitutional structure, or a change in the Japanese Government as a whole he ". . . will withhold the issuance of orders on these questions pending agreement thereon in the Far Eastern Commission."

6) But, in case of necessity the Supreme Commander could, after appropriate preliminary consideration with other members of the Council, make decisions concerning changes of individual members of the Japanese Cabinet.

This accord recommended itself to the American Government because the United States was left in a position to determine policies for the evolution of defeated Japan into a demilitarized, democratic, friendly, ultimately self-supporting nation. It was tolerable to MacArthur because it left his authority unhampered, though subject to challenge. It was acceptable to the Soviet Government because it provided protection against a deliberate attempt to convert Japan into a hostile country, and preserved the chance of influencing Japanese affairs after the occupation.

XII

The Reception of
the Moscow Accord

Byrnes was jubilant over the outcome of the conference—as evidence of his skill as defender of American interests and mediator for peace. "The man who . . . sat before a radio microphone in Washington to report to the American people was far happier than the one who had sat before the same microphone upon his return from London only fifteen weeks earlier." [1]

The moving glacier of hostility had been halted. Some subjects of contention had been settled. Others had been left over. As Byrnes remarked, "There never will be a time when all questions are settled. It was time for them to adjourn and go home." That they did, at 3:30 A.M. on the morning of December 27, after a tough tussle over the language of some parts of the public release.

As Byrnes remembered: "I was dead tired; all of us were. . . . Our airplane was scheduled to take off at 7:30. I packed, had a short nap, talked to the American newspaper and radio correspondents, and got to the airport on time." [2] In good

[1] *Speaking Frankly,* p. 121.
[2] *Ibid.*

spirits just before he boarded the plane he told the reporters that he thought the important result of the conference was the establishment of closer and cordial relations, so that the possibility of continued agreement was improved. When asked, "Are you still going strong?" he answered laughingly, "No, but I'm going." The correspondent of the Associated Press had the impression that the American Secretary was visibly touched by Mr. Molotov's gesture in coming out in the predawn cold. They exchanged firm handclasps.[3]

Bevin, by contrast, was glum, and with reason. The Russians had been readier to defy the power and test the will of exhausted Britain than to oppose the United States in its realm of primary interest. Molotov's attempts to ease or shove British forces out of Greece, leaving that country open to Communist pressure, irritated him. The grudging and unreliable concession made by the Soviet Government in regard to changes in the governments of Rumania and Bulgaria seemed to him inadequate. And above all else Molotov's refusal to set a fixed date for evacuation of Soviet troops from Iran, or even to have it stated in the official protocol that this subject had been discussed, left him worried. The continued rebuff of the British and American proposal concerning transit through the Dardanelles Straits, and continued agitation for the return to the Soviet Union of Turkish provinces that had once been in the Czarist Empire, were part of the same Soviet probing. If soft tissue was found, incision, he feared, would follow. No more than Molotov did Bevin foresee how strongly the American Government—under a snap-jawed Truman—would stand with Britain behind the governments of Iran and Turkey, when the crisis came.

Bevin's talks with Stalin had left him up in the air. He had told the Marshal (on December 19) that he wanted to carry out the British treaty of friendship and alliance with the Soviet

[3] Dispatch from Moscow, *The New York Times*, December 28, 1945.

Union in spirit, as well as in words. Stalin said he did, too. When Bevin had gone on to explain that the United Kingdom had to have some security arrangement with France and other nearby countries, just as the Soviet Union had with its neighbors, but that he was resolved not to do anything against the Soviet Government, nor to act without informing Stalin and explaining Britain's measures, Stalin had said simply, "I believe you." Nothing more.

Bevin was at times put out by Byrnes. For the Secretary of State sometimes seemed unconcerned about relations with Britain and neglectful about letting him know what he was going to say to the Russians—as when Byrnes gave a copy of the Ethridge report to Molotov before it was shown Bevin, although the British Embassy had opened its files to Ethridge. And most irritating was the fact that although only six weeks before, Truman had agreed with Prime Minister Attlee and Prime Minister Mackenzie King of Canada that they should proceed in step in the effort to work out a plan for control of atomic energy. Byrnes had brought a written proposal to this end from Washington which had not been cleared with either of these two sharers in the atomic-bomb project, and had seemed about to hand it to the Russians without discussing it with him. When Bevin remonstrated, Byrnes had allowed Bevin only two days to submit this document for consideration of the British Cabinet. Then—without waiting for British approval—the Secretary had gone ahead and presented his proposal to Molotov, an act which Bevin considered in bad faith.

Molotov was aware of the dissonance between the two men. He tried to use it to win, but with little success. For despite the gusts of cool air which blew between them, Byrnes and Bevin did stand together on all essential points. Divergences appeared in the relative importance which each attached to particular situations. But these reflected differences of presumed national interest or involvement, rather than personal feelings.

In the radio broadcast which Byrnes made on December 30, he stated that "From the outset we have planned to make the control of Japan an Allied responsibility." Then he proceeded to give a lucid account of the essential features of agreements about the Far Eastern Commission and the Allied Council. This summary ended in the affirmation that "The proposals we offered regarding Japan make it clear that we intend to cooperate with our Allies and we expect them to cooperate with us. But at the same time our agreement safeguards the efficient administration which has been set up in Japan under the Supreme Allied Commander. . . . We were determined to assure that the outstanding and efficient administration set up and executed by General MacArthur should not be obstructed." [4]

The Supreme Commander had made almost sure of that. All the while that the arrangements for the control of Japan had been under negotiation, he had made clear his opposition to any infringement on his authority, and any formal obligation even to confer with representatives of our allies about action. The instructions which had been sent to Byrnes from Washington had been mindful of MacArthur's sense that the direction of Japan was a job for one man and that he ought to be let free to do it.

The Supreme Commander seems to have suspected that the Administration might be trying to shift to him the responsibility for the agreement which was reached at Moscow. Thus when a State Department press officer stated publicly that MacArthur had been kept informed of the negotiations in Moscow and had not objected to the agreement before it was approved, the Supreme Commander issued a tart denial of this "prevarication." In this he said that "On October 31, before

[4] Department of State press release, December 30, 1945. For complete text of radio address see The Department of State Bulletin, vol. XIII, No. 340, December 30, 1945, pp. 1033–36, 1047.

the convening of the Moscow conference, my final disagreement, to such a suggested plan, was contained in my radio to the Chief of Staff for the Secretary of State advising that the terms 'in my opinion are not acceptable.' Since that time my views have not been sought." [5]

Yet he would not resign. In telling the world so, he could not help being declamatory. "It is my firm intent, within the authority entrusted to me, to try to make it [the system of control] work. . . . The issues involved are too vital to the future of the world to have them bog down. With good-will on the part of those concerned, it is my fervent hope that there will be no insuperable obstacles." He accepted the presence of Allied representatives because it was in conformity with American foreign policy, saying, "I am here to serve and not to hinder or obstruct the American Government." [6]

Subsequent events proved that he could and did master hindrances, and that he did faithfully serve both the American Government and the Japanese people.

Thorough and comprehensive evaluations of the Moscow Conference as a whole will be given us by others. But here let me contribute a few more fragmentary comments, as pertinent to an understanding of how the agreements were received and regarded.

Soviet official statements were pleasantly smooth. Whether this attitude was feigned or genuine, deceiving or self-deceiving, I do not know. Truth about the Soviet reasoning and reckoning still lies buried in the Soviet secret records, perhaps disfigured now by the scratching of editorial worms. The government newspaper, *Izvestia*, set the general tone: "The decisions of the Moscow Conference witness that a new

[5] MacArthur, *Reminiscences*, p. 292.
[6] Front page report by Lindesay Parrott, "General Denies Approving 4-Power Council for Tokyo," *The New York Times*, December 31, 1945.

step has been made toward the development of the collaboration of the Allied states"; it added that "without such collaboration there will be no stability or peace." The satisfaction of the Soviet commentators seemed to derive especially from the agreement about the control of atomic energy and the impending end of the quarrel over the governments of Rumania and Bulgaria. *Pravda* did emphasize the "great significance" of the Far Eastern Commission, and of the four-power Council for Japan. But as the correspondent for *The Christian Science Monitor* remarked, "The Russians, who are realists in such matters, doubtless realize that it [the agreement about arrangements for the control of Japan] is this moral vindication of their claim to a voice in the administration of Japan that has been achieved rather than its implementation." [7]

The appraisal of the Conference made by the *Economist* was typical of moderate English opinion. It observed that in the Far East ". . . it is the Russians who have, on the whole, made the concessions and accepted the fact of American domination," and then went on to its general conclusion—which was akin to Bevin's:

> It can thus be argued that the Moscow Conference does not represent simply a one-sided retreat but a genuine attempt at compromise. The contention is true, however, only of Russo-American relations. . . . As the smallest of the Big Three, Britain does not enjoy the independence and freedom of action of either America or Russia. The Russians are also very ready to counter what they believe to be the perennial danger of a hostile Anglo-Saxon bloc by playing one ally off against the other. In this case, owing to the inexperience of Mr. Byrnes as a negotiator and America's general diplomatic myopia when any area other

[7] Dispatch from Moscow by Edmund Stevens, "Russia Applauds Nippon Solution," *The Christian Science Monitor*, December 28, 1945, pp. 1, 3.

than the Far East is in question, the Russians have succeeded in separating their two Allies and Great Britain has been left isolated.[8]

But it was the *Economist,* I believe, which was myopic, rather than American diplomats; and American journalistic appraisals, though divided and critical, were more farsighted and sensible. I will give two of the more thoughtful examples.

Arthur Krock's summing up in *The New York Times* began, "The stalemate of London was broken and, in many respects, constructively." [9] And Joseph Harsch, in a well-considered piece in *The Christian Science Monitor* almost two weeks after the conference ended, perceived the implicit realities of the accords reached, when he wrote:

> It is to be noted, without surprise, that the settlement in the Balkans mapped out at the Moscow Conference is progressing according to the same pattern which has marked the settlement over Japan. That is to say, Russia is making superficial concessions to Western opinion in the Balkans, but without much doubt retaining the full substance of power. This was inevitable from the moment Secretary of State Byrnes explained the American concessions over Japan [as he did after his return to Washington] as in no way weakening the real substance of American authority in Japan. The two settlements were linked together at Moscow and it was inevitable that the pattern of execution established for one would be carried out in the other. . . . This does not imply that the total result is unfair—in terms of big-Power politics. . . . It has the one considerable merit of representing the abandonment of a double moral standard by both America and

[8] "Diplomatic Balance Sheet," *Economist,* January 5, 1946, pp. 2–4.
[9] From an article headed "Give and Take at the Moscow Conference," *The New York Times,* December 28, 1945, p. 14.

Russia. Up to Moscow, America was trying to apply exclusive American control to Japan, but holding out for the principle of joint responsibility and authority in the Balkans. And Russia equally, was urging joint responsibility and authority in Japan, but holding out for exclusive Russian control in the Balkans. . . . The way things are going in the Balkans has a distinct acid taste in Western mouths. But it must in fairness be recognized that prospects in Japan produce a puckering of Russian mouths.[10]

Unexpectedly, the compromises made at Moscow left a pucker in President Truman's mouth.

[10] From an editorial headed "Not Ideal, But at Least a Settlement: An Intimate Message," *The Christian Science Monitor*, January 9, 1946.

XIII

Truman Takes Offense

In telling of the President's opinion of what Byrnes had done at Moscow, I shall again be sauntering out to the circumference of this narrative of the contest over the control of Japan. Truman's judgment was adverse. Byrnes hopefully believed that the Moscow accords would bring about a surcease in the cold war, or at least enable statesmen to bring about a surcease. Truman thought the settlements made or envisaged were more to Soviet advantage than to our own, that Byrnes had been "soft on the Communists."

Truman was in Independence on December 27 when he was informed that Byrnes, just starting back from Moscow, had asked Charles Ross, the White House press secretary, to arrange for a broadcast so that he might report to the American people on the results of the conference. Truman had not yet seen the text of the protocol of the Conference, which was forwarded to him a few hours later by the State Department. Chafing under the sense that Byrnes had not kept him well informed about the measures he took at Moscow or the outcome of the discussions, he was angered at this initiative. For all he could tell, Byrnes might be intending to go ahead and give this address even before reporting to him or submitting the text of the address which he would give.

On arriving back in Washington, the President was immediately set upon by Senator Arthur H. Vandenberg, the ranking Republican member of the Foreign Relations Committee. That bustling senator, who subsequently earned renown by backing Truman's policies, was wrought up. He thought that the accord entered into by Byrnes at Moscow which contemplated the creation of a special committee of the United Nations to prepare a plan for international control of atomic energy might not be satisfactory; that the Administration might give away some of our secrets before there were adequate safeguards and controls. I have an impression—though it is no more than an impression—that this call of Vandenberg's enlivened the President's sense that Byrnes might have let him in for trouble.

Truman left the White House at once for the Presidential yacht, the *Williamsburg*. According to the President's reminiscent account of what happened next: while the *Williamsburg* was anchored at Quantico, he was informed that Byrnes, having just arrived in Washington, had again telephoned Ross to find out whether the broadcast had been arranged; and he instructed Ross to tell Byrnes "that you had better come down here posthaste and make your report. . . ." [1] But according to Byrnes' subsequent account, although dead tired, he did not wait to be summoned. He asked the White House to send a message to the President, informing him of his return and his wish to report at the President's convenience, and also stating that he expected to make a radio speech the following evening about the work of the Conference; and Truman's invitation to join him on the *Williamsburg* had quickly followed. [2]

The two first talked alone by themselves. Again the versions of what was said are so variant that the student is left to wonder whose memory either lapsed or was corrected by time. Truman wrote, "I told him that I did not like the way in

[1] *Year of Decisions*, p. 550.
[2] *Speaking Frankly*, p. 237.

which I had been left in the dark about the Moscow conference. I told him that, as President, I intended to know what progress we were making and what we were doing in foreign negotiations. I said that it was shocking that a communiqué should be issued in Washington announcing a foreign-policy development of major importance that I had never heard of. I said I would not tolerate a repetition of such conduct. Byrnes sought to put the blame mostly on his subordinates. He said that he had expected them to keep me informed. But he now admitted that he should have attended to it personally."[3] Yet according to Byrnes, "After I had reported to the President on what had happened at the conference, he expressed wholehearted approval of my action. He asked me to remain for dinner."[4]

At dinner almost all of Truman's coterie were present—Admiral William Leahy, George Allen, Major General Harry H. Vaughan, Clark Clifford, Charles Ross, Matthew Connelly, Brigadier General Wallace Graham, his physician, and Judge Samuel Rosenman. Byrnes' memory of the occasion is that at the President's request he repeated his account during dinner of what had gone on in Moscow, being interrupted from time to time by the President to express his approval. According to the Secretary of State, the only one who expressed dissatisfaction was Admiral Leahy.[5] He disliked especially the procedure for the reform of the Rumanian and Bulgarian Governments. Byrnes thought that his report had been favorably received by everyone else and that his visit ended genially. "Immediately after dinner," Byrnes' account continues, "I asked to be excused because I had to fly back to Washington; because of the rain and sleet then falling I feared a low ceiling at Wash-

[3] *Year of Decisions*, p. 550.

[4] *Speaking Frankly*, p. 237.

[5] Clark Clifford, an observant adviser, remembers that "All through dinner, Leahy, in a really effective and gentle manner to which Byrnes could not take exception, had the needle in him." Quoted in Jonathan Daniels, *The Man of Independence*, Philadelphia, J. B. Lippincott Company, 1950, p. 311.

ington. There was no further discussion of our foreign problems. The President invited me to come back New Year's Eve and spend the night on the ship, and I promised to return." [6] There is no hint of a remembered reprimand in his memoirs.

Whatever may really have happened on the *Williamsburg*, what happened afterward is clear. Truman smoldered. His judgment of what had been done at Moscow, after he had studied the documents which Byrnes had left with him, became more critical. His impression of Byrnes' performance, as caustically summed up to a confidant, was, "Byrnes lost his nerve in Moscow." [7]

The President in his *Memoirs* averred that on January 5 he read to Byrnes a letter written in longhand, setting down bluntly what he believed to be Byrnes' derelictions, and his opinion of the outcome of the Moscow Conference. In the latter regard the letter implied that Byrnes had failed to maintain the basic lines of American foreign policy and to serve its main purposes effectively. He said peremptorily, "I do not think we should play compromise any longer. We should refuse to recognize Rumania and Bulgaria until they comply with our requirements; we should let our position on Iran be known in no uncertain terms and we should continue to insist on the internationalization of the Kiel Canal, the Rhine-Danube waterway and the Black Sea Straits and we should maintain complete control of Japan and the Pacific. We should rehabilitate China and create a strong central government there. We should do the same for Korea. . . . I'm tired of babying the Soviets." [8]

Byrnes has publicly and directly denied the truth of the President's version of what occurred between them after he returned from Moscow. In particular he has written: "The statement made by the President that he read the memorandum letter to me is absolutely untrue. . . . In none of the many

[6] *Speaking Frankly*, p. 238.
[7] Daniels, *The Man of Independence*, p. 310.
[8] *Year of Decisions*, p. 552.

conversations between the President and me did he mention it. There is no possibility that I could have forgotten it."

Byrnes has further stated: "The evidence is impressive that the document was written by the President, and formally signed by him, to record himself favorably" and "I deny that it was read to me or sent to me." [8a]

Were the objectives which Truman set down as "shoulds" to be used as gauge of the success or failure of his own diplomacy in the years after the Moscow Conference, that would have to be adjudged a failure. Truman *did* recognize the governments of Bulgaria and Rumania even though our requirements were not genuinely met. The proposal for internationalization of European waterways and the Black Sea Straits —which Truman had first made at Potsdam—Stalin continued to ignore. We failed to create a strong central government in China and rehabilitate the country. The accord reached by Byrnes at Moscow which was directed toward the unification of Korea was not put into effect. In short, Truman later found he could not by huffing and puffing blow the house down. His future successes rested on military alliances and the strength of American arms.

Thus, it may be said summarily, Truman's appraisal of Byrnes' performance at Moscow was unjust. He did not acknowledge Byrnes' adroit and effective disposition of Far Eastern questions—especially the control of Japan. Nor did he remark on the relatively acceptable accord on the procedure for making peace treaties. Nor did he foresee that Byrnes' and Bevin's forceful presentations about Iran would later bring the Soviet Union to accede to a resolution of the United Nations and withdraw its troops from Iran. Nor does he seem to have appreciated that it was not possible without use of threats of force to extract from the Soviet Union a genuine and reliable relaxation of Communist control of the Balkan countries in

---

[8a] This denial and refutation were set down in detail by Byrnes in an article published in *Colliers'* April 26, 1952. The diverse supporting grounds for Byrnes' denial are to me convincing.

which Soviet troops were stationed, and that a continuance of that argument was no longer promising. Nor did he then or later validate the opinion that in presenting the plan for control of atomic energy, Byrnes had departed from his instructions. In fact, the ideas of both Truman and Byrnes in this complex matter were at this time tussocky; both overvalued what they regarded as American exclusive knowledge of how to make atomic weapons.

There is temptation to speculate further about the developments that may have turned Truman into so mordant a critic of the Moscow accords. One such development may have been a belated though unacknowledged recognition that his policy of patience and compromise at the Potsdam Conference had not checked the expansion of Soviet dominance into and over East Central Europe; another, that the way in which Stalin was dictating the political life of Poland, Bulgaria, and Rumania incensed him more and more, making a conciliatory policy seem more and more ineffective. Was he upset by rumblings of opposition, especially of senators who wanted to make the cause of the "captive nations" our own? I suspect that he feared that those Americans who were becoming disappointed by the situation emerging after the war would blame him for not fulfilling their hopes of a different world.

But it is likely that all such conceived reasons for being dissatisfied with what Byrnes did at Moscow could have been smoothed away, had the President not been affronted by what he regarded as Byrnes' negligence in informing and consulting him—as taking unto himself the authority to make final decisions which were the prerogative of the President.

Byrnes was offhand and sure of himself. He did not inform Truman each day of his talks with Molotov and Bevin in the Conference rooms, nor submit for approval each of the minor turns in the negotiations. Harriman offered to help Byrnes draft the customary daily summary to be sent to Washington. Byrnes answered—as quoted by Cabell Phillips—

"I'm not going to send any daily reports. I don't trust the White House. It leaks. And I don't want any of this coming out in the papers until I get home." [9] Byrnes, after all his many years in the Senate, was used to striking bargains first, without talking about them until they were made, and then cannily. The only regular reports made were brief daily summaries sent by the delegation about the subjects discussed and issues presented.

Byrnes' sparse reporting from Moscow is explicable, but not condonable. The two men did not have the close personal association, the easy confluence of thought, or the mutual confidence that might have made the lapse natural. Byrnes was not mindful of Truman's pride of person and lacked sufficient sense of deference to satisfy the occupant of the Presidential office—the man ultimately responsible for all decisions.

But at least twice Byrnes did send special messages to Washington. On being informed by Acheson that the President had made clear to worried Senators ". . . that any proposals advanced [about atomic energy] would be referred here before agreement was reached and that he had no intention of agreeing to disclose any information regarding the bomb at this time or unless and until arrangements for inspection and safeguards could be worked out," Byrnes answered at once [December 17], "I do not intend presenting any proposal outside of the framework of the three power declaration. . . ." [10]

Then, on the day before Christmas, after his second talk with Stalin, Byrnes sent Truman a report on the progress and status of the negotiations on all important subjects. The final paragraph ended, "The situation is encouraging and I hope that today we can reach final agreement on the questions outstanding and wind up our work tomorrow."

Truman's comment on this message in his memoirs is revealing, "This message told me very little that the newspaper

[9] *The Truman Presidency*, New York, The Macmillan Company, 1966, p. 148.
[10] Truman, *Year of Decisions*, p. 548.

correspondents had not already reported from Moscow. This was not what I considered a proper account by a Cabinet member to the President. It was more like one partner in a business telling the other that his business trip was progressing well and not to worry." [11]

Actually there was little to tell that had not been told. What Truman wanted was deference, and the chance to object or approve—at every step. He would not accord Byrnes the same freedom of judgment as he later accorded Marshall, for he did not have the same liking or admiration for him.

But, to repeat, the lapse in current reporting would not in itself have sent Truman's indignation soaring. What finally did, was that Byrnes did not trouble to consult him about the protocol before signing it, nor about the public statement (the communiqué) concerning the conference before it was released. Then Truman thought that Byrnes was going to broadcast to the American public about the conference before giving him the chance to look over the text of the radio address. This was a careless course. It ignored the fact that it was the President who would ultimately have to bear the responsibility for what was done at Moscow, live with the consequences, endure the blame, or reap the praise.

It is time to return from the circumference of my central subject and briefly observe the course of the contest over the control of Japan during the following years, when the arrangements shaped in Moscow were in operation.

[11] *Ibid.,* p. 549.

XIV

The Contest Carried On

Harriman, having resigned, since he thought he had been away from the United States too long, paid a farewell call on Stalin on January 23. Their talk touched briefly on what was happening in Japan. Stalin said that he knew very little, since General Derevyanko, who had been designated as the Soviet member of the Allied Council in Tokyo, had been held up by bad weather. He had represented his country at the Japanese surrender in September and had been suddenly recalled to Moscow in October. The bad weather in Moscow must have lasted very long, for Derevyanko did not turn up in Tokyo until spring.

What did Stalin think about the Emperor now? Harriman asked. The Marshal said he did not believe the Emperor was needed by either the Allies or the Japanese people. If the Allies wanted to see democracy in Japan and the real elimination of military influence, they ought to get rid of the Imperial institution. When Harriman went on to solicit Stalin's impressions of what MacArthur was doing in Japan, the Marshal remarked merely that he thought that the Supreme Commander's action in arresting Japanese military officers was a good thing, but that he had no information as to how the demobilization of the Japanese was going and he did not know whether the Japanese war potential was being really weakened.

Though this talk left the impression that Stalin might be willing to allow the United States to have the lead in Japan, it also showed that he still felt that the American authorities preferred to have him learn what was going on there only after the fact. This Harriman called to MacArthur's attention, when he stopped off at Tokyo on his return journey to the United States.

He read to the Supreme Commander sections of a memo he had made of the talk he had had with Stalin the previous October at Sochi. In this, it will be recalled, Stalin had said with indignation that the Soviet military commander in Japan was being treated "as a piece of furniture" and that he would not tolerate it. MacArthur refuted Stalin's charge that he had disregarded General Derevyanko. He detailed the number of their talks and his efforts to be courteous and to seek advice. Derevyanko was civil. Perhaps he was stupid, because he did not seem to understand the problems and had refrained from expressing any views. On leaving Tokyo, Derevyanko had told MacArthur that he appreciated the many courtesies which had been shown him. MacArthur thought the Russian was disturbed that he had been recalled to Moscow, and wondered whether he was worried about his personal safety.[1]

Harriman remarked that it had to be borne in mind that the Soviet Government never allowed any official to express a personal opinion. He suggested that MacArthur should continue to keep Derevyanko informed but that he should not expect him to take any responsibility. Therefore, he thought the Supreme Commander would be well advised not to delay any action longer than was justified while waiting for the Soviet member of the Council to get instructions. He tried to impress MacArthur with the usefulness of keeping the Ameri-

---

[1] I must leave to others the task of reconciling the version which MacArthur gave Harriman of his relations with Derevyanko with that contained in his *Reminiscences*, p. 285 and pp. 291-293, of which brief note is made in Chapter VI and in this chapter.

can Embassy in Moscow *au courant* with his discussions with Derevyanko so that the Embassy could see to it that Stalin was accurately informed.

MacArthur's summarizing generalization was astute: what Stalin really wanted was an extension of the wartime military alliance, a continuation of the same type of relationship that had existed during the war. This would allow the great powers to arrive at an understanding which would permit each to carry out its own operations and to attain its individual aims by whatever means were possible and through whatever forces it had at its disposal.

Though Stalin clung to his decision not to provide a contingent of Russian troops, he accepted a place on the Allied Council, and sent General Derevyanko back to Tokyo as Soviet member. The Council met frequently over the years—usually at two-week intervals—after its opening meeting in April 1946.

MacArthur was on guard lest the Council intrude upon his prerogatives. He thought it had been conceived in order to lessen his authority. At best it was to him a nuisance which often caused friction in an operation that otherwise was working smoothly, and imposed chores on his overworked staff. He was quick to conclude that the Council was trying to grasp actual exercise of control rather than limiting itself to proffering ideas and advice.

MacArthur himself attended only the first meeting of the Council. But on this occasion, without having consulted the other members, he announced that the press would be admitted to its meetings. This accorded with the general nature of his directives. It gave the Japanese the sense that the work of the occupation was being carried out in the open. However, it also provided the Soviet member with a good and continuous opportunity to get publicity for agitating statements and proposals. Now and again, members of the Western press took up Derevyanko's cause against MacArthur.

MacArthur, believing he had all he could do to direct Japanese affairs, had his deputy, George Atcheson, Jr., serve as chairman and United States member. Atcheson served as MacArthur's deputy until killed in an air crash in August, 1947. Thereafter, William J. Sebald served as his deputy and as chairman of the Commission. Each, being as well head of the Diplomatic Section of the Supreme Commander for the Allied Powers (SCAP), acted as an intermediary between the Council and the Supreme Commander. Before and after each meeting the deputy reported to MacArthur. It never was wholly clear whether the United States member was speaking for the American Government or for SCAP; but in practice the guidance came from MacArthur rather than directly from Washington.

During the early period of the Council's work a sustained attempt was made by the Supreme Commander not only to keep the other members informed but to introduce subjects for consultation and advice. But after a while, as one or another member queried or criticized some American proposal, MacArthur lost patience. From then on he discouraged all American initiatives and let the Council languish, perhaps to die by inanition.

At the start, the Soviet Government did have a legitimate interest in various matters under consideration, as for example, the extension of Japanese fishing areas and the relations between Japanese labor unions and international bodies. Derevyanko was assiduous in asking questions and in making and examining proposals at the Council meetings. He appeared at first disposed to agree in principle with what the American member favored. But this period of seeming reasonableness was brief. From July, 1946, on Derevyanko began to raise questions and make objections in the Council in order to cause trouble for the Supreme Commander rather than to improve SCAP's performance. More and more often the ideological note was injected by him into discussion of proposed internal Japanese reforms; he began to berate as a Communist rather than joust as a Russian. Several times he wrote letters to MacArthur protesting some alleged case of police brutality or other form of suppression of "democratic Japanese" and gave copies to the press before MacArthur had seen the original. The Americans formed the impression that he was engaged in a determined attempt to turn the Japanese people against both SCAP and the United States.

As Derevyanko grew more assertive, MacArthur became more dismissive and angry. His judgment of the Council hardened into hostility—which remained in his later reminiscent account. "This latter body [the Council] was, by its terms of reference, solely advisory and consultative. But it was neither the one nor the other, its sole contribution being that of nuisance and defamation."[2] He instructed the American representative in the Council not to bear Derevyanko's criticisms with patience but to take the offensive. The sessions became almost abusive.

The Soviet representative on the Security Council of the United Nations, it may be recalled, was absenting himself during the late spring of 1950. Similarly, no Soviet member of the Allied Council for Japan attended its meetings from early April of that year until early November. Then General Kislenko suddenly appeared in place of Derevyanko. By then the winds of the war in Korea were blowing furiously, and the last meeting in 1950 was an outright exchange of insults. Thereafter, until the end of 1952, the discussions in the Council were of little consequence.

In summary then, the creation of the Council for Japan did not produce cooperation or understanding between the American and Soviet Governments. Nor did it immunize Japan from the impact of the cold war. To the contrary, the arguments in the Council may have fanned the antagonism.[3]

[2] *Reminiscences*, p. 293.
[3] Students may want to compare my brief account of the vicissitudes of the Allied Council with the one given in the *Report of Government Section Supreme Commander for the Allied Powers*, pp. xix-xx. "The

The Soviet member did not succeed in disturbing the conduct of the occupation. But in various ways difficult to trace with certainty, it is probable that the currents of criticism which Derevyanko managed to stir up in the press and through the Japanese Communist party did influence in some measure the course of the "democratization" of Japan, economically and politically.

The Far Eastern Commission tried hard to get ahead with its assignments. Its members had gone to Tokyo as the Moscow Conference was ended, to consult with the Supreme Commander and to study conditions. While on its way, the Commission had been informed of the changes in its terms of reference that were agreed upon in Moscow. Thereupon it had sent a message to the Soviet Embassy in Washington, stating that the chairman and members of the Commission ". . . would welcome participation by the Soviet representative appointed to the Far Eastern Commission and his assistance in the studies and work . . . pending their return to the United States." The Soviet Government had neither accepted nor refused this invitation. It had announced that it assumed that as soon as the Commission returned to the United States, the American Government would take measures to convene what it termed "an organization session," so that it might begin to function on the basis of the decisions reached in Moscow. The necessary formal measures were taken. In February, 1946, the renovated Commission met in Washington in the unrenovated but still lovely structure which had housed the Japanese

Allied Council for Japan on the other hand, by its very terms of reference, had little potency. MacArthur endeavored following its activation to make of it a constructive force in the occupation, but as it had no responsibility for executive action, its several Allied members obviously were in no position to give material assistance. Nor could MacArthur permit it to interfere with the executive action for which he was solely responsible to the Allied Powers or countenance its meetings to be used as a sounding board for propaganda."

The collection of the verbatim minutes of most of the meetings of the Council is in the Library of Congress.

Embassy before the war. The Soviet Government named Ambassador Andrei Gromyko as its representative, and Ambassador N. V. Novikov as alternate. In the distribution of committee chairmanships, the Soviet member was designated as chairman of the committee on "strengthening of democratic tendencies."

The Soviet Government strove at once to have Gromyko appointed vice-chairman of the Commission. Just before the first formal business meeting of the reorganized Commission, Novikov tried to persuade General Frank R. McCoy, the American representative and chairman, to so propose, on the score that it would be a suitable recognition of the position of the Soviet Union, and also facilitate the work of the Commission by assuring close cooperation of their two governments.

General McCoy consulted the other members of the Commission. While that group was considering the matter, Novikov, under instructions, sought Byrnes' support for this Soviet request. Byrnes said he would have to take the matter under advisement. After talking with General McCoy he concluded that it would be inadvisable to appoint the Soviet representative as the sole vice-chairman of the Commission. Should it be necessary, he told McCoy, to have any vice-chairman, he would favor the appointment of three—the Soviet, British, and Chinese representatives.

The Soviet Government was willing to accept such an arrangement. But others opposed it. The New Zealand and Australian representatives said that they could not assent to having all three vice-chairmanships held by delegates from the nations which held the veto power. The French representative said that if there were to be three vice-chairmen, there should be four—the fourth being the French member.

Three vice-chairmen (Lord Halifax, Gromyko, and Wei Tao-ming) were approved "upon the basis of their personal qualifications." But the same differences of interests and opinions reasserted themselves. So when in July, 1946, the question of the succession of these three individuals—who had all left

Washington—came up, the Commission resolved to leave it in abeyance. Subsequently the American Government tried to persuade the Australian Government—which, backed by the British Government, was the most obdurate—to accede to the appointment of three new vice-chairmen. In an effort to reassure the Australian Government that this did not mean that Australia would not have an adequate chance to participate in decisions of policy, the American Government, in December, sent a message to Herbert V. Evatt, the Australian Foreign Minister, which stated that "the United States hopes and desires that Australia will participate on full and equal basis in the formulation of a peace treaty with Japan. . . ." But Evatt did not relax his opposition.

Whether because of this rebuff, or more probably because of differences about several important matters of policy, Novikov, the Soviet representative, who was now Ambassador to the United States, absented himself from meetings of the Commission after July. Later he also refused an invitation for New Year's Day of 1947, and when General McCoy called upon him to wish him a happy new year and to state his regrets that the Soviet representative was not continuing his early interest in the work of the Commission, Novikov said that his government was distressed at the delay in the assignment of a vice-chairmanship to the Soviet Union and that he considered it as a reflection on himself. He insisted that the American Government could overcome difficulties if it wished. But he was wrong. The Australian and New Zealand Governments continued to object, and the British Foreign Office continued to support their objections.

The episode illustrated once more the general Soviet attitude that matters of policy in regard to important issues should be decided by the two or three powers among themselves.

Throughout this whole period MacArthur bore with the Commission, though he regarded it as an unnecessary imposition—to be kept in place rather than used to contribute. One clear reason for his view of it was that it gave the Russian member a continuous chance ". . . to turn the Commission into a propaganda instrument for derogatory speeches and statements designed to obstruct orderly government in Japan." [4] He resented State Department forbearance of the Soviet member's use of the Commission to diffuse his views. On one occasion at least his restraint in public gave way. After what he regarded as a particularly vituperative speech by the Russian member, denouncing both SCAP and the Japanese Government, MacArthur made a public reply—an answer in kind. The statement, he said, had "little validity measured either by truth or realism and can be regarded as mainly a continuation of the extraordinary irresponsibility of Soviet propaganda. Its basic cause is the complete frustration of the Soviet effort to absorb Japan within the orbit of the Communistic ideology. . . . The resulting rage and frustration have produced, as in the present instance, an unbridled vulgarity of expression which is the sure hallmark of propaganda and failure. For the Soviet to prate of brutality, of labor freedom and economic liberty, is enough to make Ananias blush." [5]

An authoritative account of the Soviet efforts to influence the effort and conclusions of the Commission must await the disclosures of records still shut.[6] So merely as indicative of the pull and tug that occurred within it, I shall tell summarily of the course of argument over two major issues.

The first had to do with the date for the holding of elections for a new Japanese Diet. This defined itself as a question of jurisdiction between the Supreme Commander and the Far Eastern Commission. Was the decision one of basic policy or

[4] *Reminiscences,* p. 292.

[5] *Ibid.,* p. 293.

[6] There are, however, reliable and informative studies of the work of the Commission. Of these I would commend particularly the one written by Dr. George H. Blakeslee, *The Far Eastern Commission. A Study in International Cooperation: 1945 to 1952,* Far Eastern Series 60, Department of State Publication 5138, Washington, D.C., 1953. Also useful is Baron E. J. Lewe Van Adward, *Japan: From Surrender to Peace,* The Hague, M. Nijhoff, 1953.

merely one of execution of basic policy?

The Soviet representative, Novikov, thought it was a matter of basic policy. He averred it would be premature to hold the elections on a date as early as the one the Supreme Commander had scheduled—April 10, 1946. His argument was that this would not allow time for the liberal and democratic parties in Japan to develop their organization and strength and that therefore the result would favor the reactionary parties. The French and Chinese members sided with him. MacArthur's reply to the Commission's memorandum was both incisive and decisive. It read in part:

> The present Diet is completely unsatisfactory because of its war attaint and its unrepresentative character, having been elected in 1942 under Tojo's control. It is imperative that a more representative body be organized at the earliest possible date. . . . Every candidate for the New Diet, of whom there are over 3,000, has been screened. . . . Many reforms in the electoral system have been accomplished. . . . It is probable that the new Diet will be the most truly responsive body to the will of the people that has ever served Japan. . . . There is no ground for supposition that the reactionary party will secure a greater advantage as a result of the election at this time than at a later date. . . . Any postponement would certainly be misunderstood by the Japanese People, and would have a profound adverse reaction upon the purposes and success of the occupation. Should the results of the election prove disadvantageous to the purposes of the occupation, [it is always within the power of SCAP to require] . . . a new election. . . .[7]

[7] MacArthur's communication was distributed to the Commission on March 29, 1946. *Activities of the Far Eastern Commission*, Report by the Secretary General, February 26, 1946–July 10, 1947, Department of State Publication 2888, Washington, D. C., 1947, pp. 59–61.

Novikov continued to maintain that the matter was one of policy and not of administrative detail. But his colleagues decided that plans for holding the election had advanced so far that the decision of the Supreme Commander should not or could not be overruled. Thus it took no action. The election was held on time.

The other issue concerned the most important single question dealt with by the Far Eastern Commission during the first two years of its existence—the formulation and adoption of a new constitution.

The former constitution had enabled the military and industrial elements and the court circle to rule Japan. The Potsdam Declaration stated in part that "The Japanese Government shall remove all obstacles to the revival and strengthening of democratic tendencies among the Japanese people. Freedom of speech, of religion, and of thought, as well as respect for the fundamental human rights shall be established." And it contemplated that the occupying forces would remain until ". . . there has been established in accordance with the freely expressed will of the Japanese people a peacefully inclined and responsible government."

The ensuing effort to write a constitution for such a government brought out markedly different sets of opinions. The Supreme Commander, the American Government and the Far Eastern Commission each had its own views in regard to the proper methods for developing the constitution, the competence of the Commission to pass upon its terms, and the procedure for adopting it. The views of the Supreme Commander and the Commission regarding their respective authority in all these matters were sharply conflicting and never were wholly resolved. The field of decision was complex, the discussions involving so many governments even more complex, the crossing swirls of argument as hard to follow as the waves in a breeez-blown sea. So any brief account must be like a snapshot from which the background has been rubbed out.

The Supreme Commander had lost no time in fathering a new constitution. In the Potsdam Declaration, in the terms of surrender, and in the initial directives, there was authority and a mandate to hurry. So he had not waited for the Far Eastern Commission to be formed, nor deemed it necessary to consult any foreign government. In the month of surrender (September, 1945) he had directed the Japanese Prime Minister, Prince Higashi-Kuni, to draft a plan for revision of the constitution which should permit the formation of the kind of government and society envisaged. A month later he had advised the new Prime Minister, Baron Shidehara, that the Japanese Government must revise its preliminary ideas. During that first autumn, MacArthur and his political adviser, George Atcheson, had many personal conferences with Japanese state ministers in order to help them to grasp the principles which were to guide the revision. The text of the basic provisions which the American Government believed should be incorporated in the new constitution were set forth anew in an instruction which the Secretary of State sent MacArthur on October 17.

The Japanese authorities had been going forward with the task when in December, 1945, the three Foreign Ministers at Moscow reached agreement about the revised terms of reference for the Far Eastern Commission.[8] These could be construed as meaning that the Commission itself was to formulate the basic principles of the constitution, or at least approve them. When in January, 1946, therefore, the Commission visited Tokyo, the Supreme Commander assumed the attitude that the question of constitutional reform had been taken out of his hands by the Moscow Agreement which had set up the Far Eastern Commission. He had therefore briefly ceased to press the purpose.

However, the American Government quickly developed

[8] Particularly Paragraph II, defining the functions of the Far Eastern Commission. See Appendix 7.

an important new policy paper which set forth anew its views as to the constitutional reforms which the occupation authorities should insist be carried out in Japan.[9] This was sent to MacArthur for his guidance, as a directive. But circumstances as well as inclination caused him to treat it as controlling. Suffice it to say that the policy of this paper was a comprehensive plan for a democratic system of representative government, with strong safeguards of individual liberties and the rules of equality under law. Naturally, it was an expression of American ideas of how genuine political democracy could be established and maintained.

MacArthur was convinced that all efforts should be made to lead the Japanese authorities to stencil, among themselves, a constitution which fitted these principles. The American Government had said in this same policy paper that "Only as a last resort should the Supreme Commander order the Japanese Government to effect the . . . listed reforms, as the knowledge that they had been imposed by the Allies would materially reduce the possibility of their acceptance and support by the Japanese people for the future." [10]

Yet within a fortnight MacArthur felt impelled to inform the Japanese committee that its latest proposals were unacceptable, since they failed to effect the required liberalization and democratization of the constitution. Therewith, SCAP provided a text that was blunt and incisive. One of its stipulations was that the Emperor was to function only as a constitutional sovereign, responsible to the people. Another basic one—previously approved by the Prime Minister—was that "Japan renounces it [war] as an instrumentality for settling its disputes or even for preserving its own security. . . . No Jap-

[9] The paper was entitled "Reform of the Japanese Governmental System," SWNCC (State-War-Navy Coordinating Committee) 288, approved January 7, 1946. For more details see Blakeslee's *The Far Eastern Commission*, pp. 45–46.

[10] *Ibid.*, Blakeslee.

anese Army, Navy or Air Force will ever be authorized and no rights of belligerency will ever be conferred upon any Japanese force." [11]

By March 6, 1946, the Japanese Cabinet had completed a rewritten text for a constitution which the Supreme Commander thought entirely satisfactory. On that same afternoon he announced publicly, "It is with a sense of deep satisfaction that I am able today to announce a decision of the Emperor and Government of Japan to submit to the Japanese people a new and enlightened constitution which has my full approval." [12]

The ensuing discussion brought out various dissenting opinions and proposals. When in the summer of 1946 the Far Eastern Commission was in the last stages of discussion of a statement of "Basic Principles of a New Japanese Constitution" (which followed closely the policy paper of January 7, 1946) the Soviet member proposed a series of amendments. Among them were provisions for a unicameral legislature and an elected judiciary. These were rejected as inadvisable. He also urged the adoption of another series of amendments, which included a guarantee of the right to work, the eight-hour working day, prohibition of child labor, state social insurance, free medical help, and old-age care. These were rejected as being acts that might be taken later by the Japanese Government in accord with general principles contained in the constitution rather than as constitutional provisions.

The Soviet member nevertheless concurred in the statement which the Commission thereupon sent to the Supreme

[11] *Ibid.*, p. 46. General MacArthur in subsequent testimony at the joint hearings of the Senate Armed Services and Foreign Relations Committees recounted, however, that such a provision was first proposed to him by the Japanese Prime Minister, and that the Japanese authorities wrote it into the constitution of their own volition, with his encouragement.

[12] The complete text of the statement is in *The Occupation of Japan: Policy and Progress*, Far Eastern Series 17, Department of State Publication 2671, Washington, D. C., 1946, p. 132.

Commander as a directive. MacArthur objected to its publication on the ground that the Japanese people would revolt against any reforms they thought were imposed upon them, rather than a free expression of their will. The Commission refrained from releasing it.

Next the question was posed whether the Commission had to pass upon the new constitution. The American member agreed with the Soviet member and a majority of the others that the Commission had the duty to determine whether it was consistent with the Potsdam Declaration and other controlling documents. But was positive approval by the Commission of the constitution necessary? If so the Soviet (or British or Chinese) representative could by veto delay its adoption indefinitely. The American Government therefore stood firmly behind MacArthur in his objection to such a requirement. A solution accepted by the majority provided that the constitution could be adopted by the Japanese authorities unless the Commission found it inconsistent with governing principles and texts. This would have enabled the American Government to overcome obstruction by the Commission.

SCAP accepted some other suggestions of the Commission; and the Commission took heed of SCAP's contention that "To attempt to force perfection in detail, among several democratic alternatives against Japanese objectors, would vitiate our very aim and purpose to secure adoption of a constitution which expresses the free will of the Japanese people." [13]

But the question remained as to whether the constitution could or should be adopted by the Diet and made effective *before* the Commission had passed upon it. The American Government had concurred in the resolution of the Commission of March 20, which stated ". . . the Commission desires that the Supreme Commander for the Allies make clear to the Japanese Government that the Far Eastern Commission must be given an opportunity to pass upon the final draft of the Constitu-

[13] Message from MacArthur to Commission, July 30, 1946. (Blakeslee, *The Far Eastern Commission*, p. 57.)

tion . . . before it is finally approved by the Diet and be-
comes legally valid." [14] But MacArthur objected to the postponement. Whether by coincidence or informal arrangement,
the Diet delayed formal action on the constitution long
enough to enable the Commission to complete consideration of
it.

In its final discussion of the subject in September, 1946, all
members except the Soviet representative expressed qualified
approval. The Soviet representative maintained that it was
unsatisfactory. The new Japanese constitution was adopted by
the Diet on October, 1946, and promulgated in November.

When in 1949 the Soviet representative argued that the
Commission had the duty of reviewing the operation of the
constitution, the American Government maintained that such
a review was unnecessary and highly inadvisable. Its chief
reasons—and they were sound—were that the constitution was
fulfilling well the terms of the controlling agreements and that
"The Japanese people should be encouraged to regard the
Constitution as their own and any detraction from that feeling
should be scrupulously avoided."

By this time almost all members of the Commission had
become satisfied with the constitution. Even the Australian
member tended to concur that it had worked reasonably well
and there was little need to change it. The final comment of
the Soviet representative was that while he believed the constitution "could have been improved in the direction of its
further democratization, it [the Soviet delegation] nevertheless
considered that at the present time the essential question to be
dealt with was not so much the review of the Constitution as
the fact that even those few democratic provisions which were
contained in it were being systematically violated by the
United States occupation authorities and by the Japanese
Government. . . ." [15]

[14] *Ibid.*
[15] *Ibid.*, p. 65.

But this denunciation did not derive mainly, I believe, from differences over what was being done in Japan. It was rather just one of the many expressions of the fact that in the years between 1946 and 1948 the cold war had set in and hardened into an outright and worldwide test of influence and power.

During this period the attitude and forethought of the American Government in regard to Japan changed in rhythm with the course of the struggle against Communism in Europe. American policies regarding the economic recovery of Japan and its prospective place among the nations swiveled. Thus, for example, the United States began to encourage rather than to confine the restoration of Japanese industry. Moreover, it advocated that in the interim before a peace treaty was made, Japan should be accorded a large measure of the rights of independence in both domestic and foreign matters that would presumably be obtained by treaty.

Not only the Soviet Government, but other members of the Commission, were hesitant about such a quick and extensive release of Japan. Their animosity had not faded as fast or as far as ours; in China, the Philippines, Australia, and New Zealand fear and hatred of the Japanese lasted longer. It did not yield as readily to the wish to be sure that Japan would be aligned against Communism.

For by this time most Americans were inclining toward the belief that if in the future any country in the Far East should be feared as an aggressor it was the Soviet Union rather than Japan. This fostered the judgment that it was only prudent to enable Japan to regain strength in order that it might better be able to defend itself, if need be, against Soviet subversion or attack. In the preliminary thought about a peace treaty with Japan which would end the occupation, American officials conceived that the treaty would be supplemented by an alliance and arrangements for the maintenance of an American military base in Japan.

Moreover, the American Government thought that by

then it was not only safe but necessary to end or greatly ease the exclusions and restrictions that were retarding Japan's economic recovery under a system of capitalism. It wanted to be able to reduce or discontinue the large financial contribution it was making in and for Japan. But the Soviet Government was not perturbed by the prolongation of Japan's difficulties. And various of our other former allies were afraid of the revival of Japanese commercial competition.

Because of these divergences, the tendency developed within the American Government to look upon the Far Eastern Commission—not only the Soviet Government—as an obstacle to the pursuit of American aims. Washington, as well as MacArthur, was inclined to circumvent it or disregard its complaints. The Soviet Government was among the leading protesters of this inattention.

The cold war was on. The meetings of the Commission grew less and less frequent. After a critical dispute within the Commission about authorizing the visitations and stationing of Japanese agents abroad and Japanese participation in international conferences, the Soviet Government, in June, 1950, withdrew. This was the end of the Soviet attempt to contest the control of Japan in and through the Far Eastern Commission.

By this time, officials of the Japanese and American Governments were deeply engaged in consideration of the terms of the treaty of peace. These had been carried far before any foreign government was admitted into consultation.

The Soviet Government remained critical of our initiative. It was taking up the flourishing cause of Communism everywhere else in the Far East. The Chinese National Government had been compelled to take refuge in Taiwan and the Soviet Government was forming a close liaison with the Chinese Communists and providing them with assistance. While foiling the efforts of the United Nations to find ways of unifying the administration of all of Korea, it was training and equipping divisions of North Korean troops.

Possibly the anticipation that the United States would proceed, despite Soviet opposition, to negotiate a preace treaty with Japan whereunder it would retain Japan as an ally, influenced the Soviet Union to support the invasion of South Korea in June, 1950. The chance seemed to offer itself to offset our alliance by encircling Japan with Communist power. With the Soviet Union looming from the north, a great Communist China on the mainland, and a Communist Korea just across the narrow waters of the Sea of Japan, even the combined American and Japanese influences in the Far East might wane. The Soviet authorities at the time may well have reckoned that, by the dual arts of subversion and propaganda and the attractions of trade and the force of geographical proximity, the Communist associates could quickly reverse the result of the struggle for the control of Japan.

In the Potsdam Declaration—the basis of the Japanese surrender—it had been envisaged that the period of occupation would be maintained only until the "new order described in the Declaration is established and until there is convincing proof that Japan's war-making power is destroyed. . . ." Once these basic objectives were achieved it had been conceived that relations would be determined by a treaty of peace.

By July, 1947, the American Government had concluded that enough progress had been made to warrant the preparation of a peace treaty. It proposed that the Far Eastern Commission convene a conference of officials and experts for the purpose. But the Chinese Nationalist Government objected to the procedure. So did the Soviet Government, more obdurately, contending that the treaty should be considered first by the Council of Foreign Ministers—China replacing France for the assignment. This would have given both a veto over every provision of the treaty.

Behind the argument over procedure that went on

through 1948 into 1949 were differences of purposes and desires. Would the treaty permit Japan freedom to enter into political and military alliances—probably with the West—or require it to be neutral? More specifically would it permit the Allies (or the United States) to maintain forces and bases in Japan? Would it permit Japan to combat external propaganda and internal subversion?

The American Government had hesitated to force the issue. It was uncertain about the durability of a treaty to which the Soviet Union and Communist China did not subscribe. Then, and not to be ignored, Japanese opinion, both official and public, seemed to prefer to wait until a treaty could be negotiated to which all Allies were parties. One strong faction, led by the Socialist Party, did not want Japan to become aligned with the United States in the cold war, maintaining that if Japan met American terms and wishes, the Soviet Union would be permanently hostile, and Japan might end up an atomic battleground. In contrast, the ruling groups of which Prime Minister Yoshida was the leading advocate, argued that Japan should and must accept whatever decision the Allies reached regarding participation in the peace treaty; that a peace treaty with some was better than no peace treaty, and would lead quickly to other settlements. By 1950 this group reached the conclusion that Japan, because of its exposed position and unarmed state, had to have allies even though it might become directly involved in the cold war. A closeness between American and Japanese authorities developed during the Korean experience that created a firm will on both sides to proceed without Soviet or Chinese participation, if need be.

But during the first months of the war in Korea there had been a division of counsel within the American government. Secretary of Defense Louis Johnson wanted to postpone initiative while the war was on. MacArthur and the State Department wished for the same reason to go forward. Johnson and the Joint Chiefs of Staff were not wholly satisfied with the security provisions which the State Department intended to propose. But MacArthur approved them once the United Nations position along the 38th parallel was assured. Then the American Government resumed the initiative with fresh vigor and determination. The Japanese Government, as well as the American, had come to regard the Chinese Communists as a threatening opponent, and did not want them to be a signatory of the peace treaty. The question of Japan's future relations with China and the Soviet Union, it was agreed, would necessarily have to be left for determination by Japan itself in the exercise of the sovereign and independent status contemplated by the treaty.

After continuous and patient discussions between American and Japanese officials, and among the Allies, and in the FEC, fifty-one nations met at San Francisco in September, 1951, to conclude and sign the treaty with Japan.

"We meet," President Truman truthfully remarked in his opening address, "to restore our former enemy to the community of peaceful nations." The terms of the treaty which were presented to the Conference reflected this intention. The full sovereignty of the Japanese people was recognized. But Japan renounced all its imperial territories as stipulated in the Potsdam Declaration. It promised to conduct itself in accordance with the principles of the United Nations Charter and to settle all international disputes by peaceful means. In one article it renounced in conclusive language the use of all offensive force. Yet—and this above all caused the Soviet Government to remain opposed—another article stipulated that Japan as a sovereign nation would possess what Article 5 of the United Nations Charter referred to as "the inherent right of self-defense." And the American and Japanese Governments made plain their intention to enter quickly into a treaty of mutual security, whereunder the United States would maintain armed forces and bases in Japan.

The Soviet representatives at the Peace Conference railed against this and various other provisions of the treaty. But at this Conference, unlike those about the European peace treaties, the Soviet Union could not use rules of procedure to prevent or deflect decision. For the terms of reference of the Conference, composed by the American and British Governments and adopted by the Conference, had been drawn with a determination that no one participant or small group of participants should be able to stall the work of the Conference or defeat the wishes of the many allies. Secretary of State Acheson, as presiding officer of the Conference, maintained these rules against all efforts to subvert or circumvent them, sometimes brusquely, sometimes even reprimandingly, while the Soviet representatives writhed.

It was left mainly to John Foster Dulles, who had done much of the extensive preliminary negotiations, to expound American views and refute Soviet objections. Some of these charges concerned the procedure by which the treaty was prepared. Others alleged that it was in violation of the Potsdam Declaration and other international accords. These were essentially arguments about the meaning and pertinence of texts; Dulles was a master of this sort of debate. One Soviet contention was that real peace in the Far East was not possible without the participation of Communist China; this was denied, on the score that the treaty showed careful regard for the interests of China, and that since "total" peace was not then possible, it was advisable to secure the very large measure of peace that was in sight. Still other Soviet complaints were that although the treaty stipulated that Formosa and the Pescadores islands were to be taken from Japan, it did not definitely state that they would be returned to China; and similarly, while it stipulated that southern Sakhalin and the Kurile Islands were to be detached from Japan, it did not definitely provide that they should be handed over to the Soviet Union.

Soviet dissatisfaction really centered on the fact that the treaty did not debar Japan from entering into a military or political alliance with the United States and other Western

Allies. In disproof of Soviet charges that the United States was restoring Japanese militarism, the American representatives pointed out that Japan had been so completely disarmed that it did not even have as yet an adequate coast guard or domestic police force. The prospect that Japan would enter into a military accord with the United States wherewith American military bases would be maintained in Japan was openly admitted. But the Americans denied that this was in contravention of the Potsdam Accord. Our answer was: "The United States has told Japan that it is prepared to station some armed forces in Japan at Japan's request so that, on the coming in force of the peace treaty, Japan will not be a total vacuum of power. The arrangement would in essence be comparable to those between other free countries which want to combine forces and facilities for the puposes of collective security. Such arrangements constitute an exercise of sovereignty, not a derogation of authority." [16]

The American Government was justified in its contention that the treaty was not unfair or injurious to the Soviet Union and Communist China or restrictive of Japanese economic recovery. The Soviet Government was correct in its perception that the mutual security arrangement allowed by the treaty would be of great protective value to the United States (and its Western allies) and Japan. Its existence has been, I believe, a healthy restraint on the thrust of the Soviet Union in Europe and of Communist China in the Far East. Over the years it has sustained the democracy and independence of

[16] This is a quotation from one of the answers to Soviet charges made by John Foster Dulles upon request of *The New York Times* on September 3, 1951, the day before the Conference opened. The full text of his answer is printed in *International Organization and Conference* (Department of State Publication 4371, Far Eastern Series 2, Washington, D. C.), along with the text of the Peace Treaty, the Terms of Reference of the Conference, and the addresses made by President Truman, Secretary Acheson, and Dulles himself. A more thorough knowledge of the range and substance of the contention can be obtained by study of the day-by-day proceedings of the Conference.

Japan. And since, traditionally, Japanese radicals have tended to regard the Russians as a dominating power and the Chinese —including the Chinese Communists—as akin, victims of Russian imperialism, the Soviet authorities should be content that they were not able to weaken or obstruct the peace treaty concluded in 1951.

The signing of the peace treaty, followed by the repulse of the invasion of South Korea and the inpressive improvement and stability of Japan caused Soviet hopes in the contest over Japan to droop. The Soviet authorities decided to bury their plans beneath the frost line, waiting for American determination to melt and Japanese memories to fade. They changed their manner toward Japan and their tactics of attraction. The Japanese cautiously responded.

Since Stalin's death in 1953 the American and Soviet Governments have been professing a mutual wish to tolerate each other and lessen the mutual strain and animosity. At present their apprehension about a nuclear-armed Communist China seems to be mitigating their rivalries for influence and clashes over ideology in Asia, except over Vietnam. Japan would like to procure the return of some of the islands off its northern coasts as a token or proof of the Soviet wish for its friendship; and the Soviet Union perceives possibilities of improving its position in Asia vis-à-vis not only Japan but China as well.

In August, 1966, Andrei Gromyko, now Soviet Foreign Minister, who twenty years before was one of the Soviet officials who accused the United States of wanting to turn Japan into an American satellite, hostile to the Soviet Union, completed a remarkable agreement with the Japanese Government. In a joint communiqué the two governments announced that their countries would strive to develop their relations in every field despite "different political creeds and social conditions." To that end they agreed to confer regularly not only about issues between them but also about international questions.

This eventuality attests to the genuineness of the American professions which have been reviewed. Insistently, repeatedly, in answer to Soviet accusations, the American Government stated that its policies were directed toward the emergence of a democratized, peaceful, and independent Japan. Events have validated its avowals. Is it too much to hope the Soviet Government will not use the chance left by our treatment of Japan to try its utmost to disturb the social order in that country and alienate it from the United States? Must the contest, now going on in acceptable ways, again turn into a fierce struggle for opposed purposes? Or in their relations with Japan can American and Soviet interests and aspirations coexist?

Deep down in their pits the thermonuclear weapons wait to wipe out the nations if they do not control their quarrels. That would be in deadly mockery of the professions of all contestants. If any records remained of ideals and interests, discussions and stratagems, such as are recounted in this narrative, they would be but the shrouds of paper in which peoples were embalmed. If the historian of our times does not put down his pencil he may turn into either a tragicomedian or a Fundamentalist preacher.

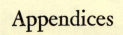

Appendices

APPENDIX 1

The Cairo Declaration

UNITED STATES OF AMERICA:
PRESIDENT ROOSEVELT
CHINA: GENERALISSIMO CHIANG KAI-SHEK
UNITED KINGDOM: PRIME MINISTER
CHURCHILL

STATEMENT RELEASED DECEMBER 1, 1943

The several military missions have agreed upon future military operations against Japan. The Three Great Allies expressed their resolve to bring unrelenting pressure against their brutal enemies by sea, land, and air. This pressure is already rising.

The Three Great Allies are fighting this war to restrain and punish the aggression of Japan. They covet no gain for themselves and have no thought of territorial expansion. It is their purpose that Japan shall be stripped of all the islands in the Pacific which she had seized or occupied since the beginning of the first World War in 1914, and that all the territories Japan has stolen from the Chinese, such as Manchuria, Formosa, and the Pescadores, shall be restored to the Republic of China. Japan will also be expelled from all other territories which she has taken by violence and greed. The aforesaid three great powers, mindful of the enslavement of the people of Korea, are determined that in due course Korea shall become free and independent.

With these objects in view the three Allies, in harmony with those of the United Nations at war with Japan, will continue to persevere in the serious and prolonged operations necessary to procure the unconditional surrender of Japan.

APPENDIX 2

AGREEMENT REGARDING JAPAN

Between the leaders of the Three Great Powers—the United States of America, the Union of Soviet Socialist Republics, and the United Kingdom of Great Britain and Northern Ireland.

Signed at Yalta February 11, 1945

The leaders of the three great powers—the Soviet Union, the United States of America and Great Britain—have agreed that in two or three months after Germany has surrendered and the war in Europe has terminated, the Soviet Union shall enter into the war against Japan on the side of the Allies on conditions that:

1) The status quo in Outer Mongolia (the Mongolian People's Republic) shall be preserved;

2) The former rights of Russia violated by the treacherous attack of Japan in 1904 shall be restored, viz:

(a) the southern part of Sakhalin as well as the islands adjacent to it shall be returned to the Soviet Union;

(b) the commercial port of Dairen shall be internationalized, the pre-eminent interests of the Soviet Union in this port being safe-guarded and the lease of Port Arthur as a naval base of the U.S.S.R. restored;

(c) the Chinese-Eastern Railroad and the South-Manchurian Railroad, which provide an outlet to Dairen, shall be jointly operated by the establishment of a joint Soviet-Chinese company, it being understood that the pre-eminent interests of the Soviet Union shall be safeguarded and that China shall retain full sovereignty in Manchuria;

3) The Kurile islands shall be handed over to the Soviet Union.

It is understood that the agreement concerning Outer Mongolia and the ports and railroads referred to above will require concurrence of Generalissimo Chiang Kai-shek. The President will take measures in order to obtain this concurrence on advice from Marshal Stalin.

The heads of the three great powers have agreed that these claims of the Soviet Union shall be unquestionably fulfilled after Japan has been defeated.

For its part, the Soviet Union expresses its readiness to conclude with the National Government of China a pact of friendship and alliance between the U.S.S.R. and China in order to render assistance to China with its armed forces for the purpose of liberating China from the Japanese yoke.

JOSEPH V. STALIN
FRANKLIN D. ROOSEVELT
WINSTON S. CHURCHILL

APPENDIX 3: Proclamation Defining Terms For Japanese Surrender

POTSDAM DECLARATION

PROCLAMATION BY THE HEADS OF
GOVERNMENTS OF THE UNITED STATES,
UNITED KINGDOM, AND CHINA

JULY 26, 1945

(1) We—the President of the United States, the President of the National Government of the Republic of China, and the Prime Minister of Great Britain, representing the hundreds of millions of our countrymen, have conferred and agree that Japan shall be given an opportunity to end this war.

(2) The prodigious land, sea and air forces of the United States, the British Empire and of China, many times reinforced by their armies and air fleets from the west, are poised to strike the final blows upon Japan. This military power is sustained and inspired by the determination of all the allied Nations to prosecute the war against Japan until she ceases to resist.

(3) The result of the futile and senseless German resistance to the might of the aroused free peoples of the world stands forth in awful clarity as an example to the people of Japan. The might that now converges on Japan is immeasurably greater than that which,

when applied to the resisting Nazis, necessarily laid waste to the lands, the industry and the method of life of the whole German people. The full application of our military power, backed by our resolve, *will* mean the inevitable and complete destruction of the Japanese armed forces and just as inevitably the utter devastation of the Japanese homeland.

(4) The time has come for Japan to decide whether she will continue to be controlled by those self-willed militaristic advisers whose unintelligent calculations have brought the Empire of Japan to the threshold of annihilation, or whether she will follow the path of reason.

(5) Following are our terms. We will not deviate from them. There are no alternatives. We shall brook no delay.

(6) There must be eliminated for all time the authority and influence of those who have deceived and misled the people of Japan into embarking on world conquest, for we insist that a new order of peace, security and justice will be impossible until irresponsible militarism is driven from the world.

(7) Until such a new order is established *and* until there is convincing proof that Japan's war-making power is destroyed, points in Japanese territory to be designated by the Allies shall be occupied to secure the achievement of the basic objectives we are here setting forth.

(8) The terms of the Cairo Declaration shall be carried out and Japanese sovereignty shall be limited to the islands of Honshu, Hokkaido, Kyushu, Shikoku and such minor islands as we determine.

(9) The Japanese military forces, after being completely disarmed, shall be permitted to return to their homes with the opportunity to lead peaceful and productive lives.

(10) We do not intend that the Japanese shall be enslaved as a race or destroyed as a nation, but stern justice shall be meted out to all war criminals, including those who have visited cruelties upon our prisoners. The Japanese Government shall remove all obstacles to the revival and strengthening of democratic tendencies among the Japanese people. Freedom of speech, of religion, and of thought, as well as respect for the fundamental human rights shall be established.

(11) Japan shall be permitted to maintain such industries as will

sustain her economy and permit the exaction of just reparations in kind, but not those which would enable her to re-arm for war. To this end, access to, as distinguished from control of, raw materials shall be permitted. Eventual Japanese participation in world trade relations shall be permitted.

(12) The occupying forces of the Allies shall be withdrawn from Japan as soon as these objectives have been accomplished and there has been established in accordance with the freely expressed will of the Japanese people a peacefully inclined and responsible government.

(13) We call upon the government of Japan to proclaim now the unconditional surrender of all Japanese armed forces, and to provide proper and adequate assurances of their good faith in such action. The alternative for Japan is prompt and utter destruction.

APPENDIX 4

REPLY BY SECRETARY OF STATE TO JAPANESE QUALIFIED ACCEPTANCE

[OF TERMS OF SURRENDER STATED IN
POTSDAM DECLARATION]

AUGUST 11, 1945

Sir:

I have the honor to acknowledge receipt of your note of August 10, and in reply to inform you that the President of the United States has directed me to send to you for transmission by your Government [the Swiss Government, which was acting as intermediary] to the Japanese Government the following message on behalf of the Governments of the United States, the United Kingdom, the Union of Soviet Socialist Republics, and China:

"With regard to the Japanese Government's message accepting the terms of the Potsdam proclamation but containing the statement, 'with the understanding that the said declaration does not comprise any demand which prejudices the prerogatives of His Majesty as a sovereign ruler,' our position is as follows:

"From the moment of surrender the authority of the Emperor and the Japanese Government to rule the state shall be subject to the Supreme Commander of the Allied powers who will take such steps as he deems to effectuate the surrender terms.

"The Emperor will be required to authorize and ensure the signature by the Government of Japan and the Japanese Imperial General Headquarters of the surrender terms necessary to carry out the provisions of the Potsdam Declaration, and shall issue his commands to all the Japanese military, naval and air authorities and to all the forces under their control wherever located to cease active operations and to surrender their arms, and to issue such other orders as the Supreme Commander may require to give effect to the surrender terms.

"Immediately upon the surrender the Japanese Government shall transport prisoners of war and civilian internees to places of safety, as directed, where they can quickly be placed aboard Allied transports.

The ultimate form of government of Japan shall, in accordance with the Potsdam Declaration, be established by the freely expressed will of the Japanese people.

"The armed forces of the Allied Powers will remain in Japan until the purposes set forth in the Potsdam Declaration are achieved."

Accept, Sir, the renewed assurance of my highest consideration.

JAMES F. BYRNES
Secretary of State

MR. MAX GRÄSSLI
Chargé d'affaires ad interim of Switzerland.

APPENDIX 5

Demobilization Directive

OFFICE OF THE SUPREME COMMANDER FOR THE ALLIED POWERS

2 SEPTEMBER 1945.

Directive
Number 1

Pursuant to the provisions of the Instrument of Surrender signed by the representatives of the Emperor of Japan and the Japanese Imperial Government and of the Japanese Imperial General Headquarters, 2 September 1945, the attached "General Order Number 1, Military and Naval" and any necessary amplifying instructions, will be issued without delay to Japanese and Japanese-controlled Armed Forces and to affected civilian agencies, for their full and complete compliance.

By direction of the Supreme Commander for the Allied Powers:

(s) R. K. Sutherland.
(t) R. K. Sutherland,
    Lieutenant General, U. S. Army,
    Chief of Staff.

1 Incl:

General Order No. 1,
Military and Naval.

GENERAL ORDER NO. 1

Military and Naval

1. The Imperial General Headquarters by direction of the Emperor, and pursuant to the surrender to the Supreme Commander for the Allied Powers of all Japanese Armed Forces by the Emperor, hereby orders all of its Commanders in Japan and abroad to cause the Japanese Armed Forces and Japanese-controlled Forces under their command to cease hostilities at once, to lay down their arms, to remain in their present locations and to surrender unconditionally to Commanders acting on behalf of the United States, the Republic of China, the United Kingdom and the British Empire, and the Union of Soviet Socialist Republics, as indicated hereafter or as may be further directed by the Supreme Commander for the Allied Powers. Immediate contact will be made with the indicated Commanders, or their designated representatives, subject to any changes in detail prescribed by the Supreme Commander for the Allied Powers, and their instructions will be completely and immediately carried out.

(a) The senior Japanese Commanders and all ground, sea, air and auxiliary forces within China (excluding Manchuria), Formosa, and French Indo-China North of 16 degrees North latitude, shall surrender to Generalissimo Chiang Kai-shek.

(b) The senior Japanese Commanders and all ground, sea, air and auxiliary forces within Manchuria, Korea North of 38 degrees North latitude, Karafuto, and the Kurile Islands, shall surrender to the Commander in Chief of Soviet Forces in the Far East.

(c) (1) The senior Japanese Commanders and all ground, sea, air and auxiliary forces within the Andamans, Nicobars, Burma, Thailand, French Indo-China South of 16 degrees North latitude, Malaya, Sumatra, Java, Lesser Sundas (including Bali, Lombok, and Timor) Boeroe, Ambon, Aroe, Tanimbar, and islands in the

Arafura Sea, Celebes, Halmahera and Dutch New Guinea shall surrender to the Supreme Allied Commander, South East Asia Command.

(2) The senior Japanese Commanders and all ground, sea, air and auxiliary forces within Borneo, British New Guinea, the Bismarcs and the Solomons shall surrender to the Commander in Chief, Australian Military Forces.

(d) The senior Japanese Commanders and all ground, sea, air and auxiliary forces in the Japanese mandated Islands, Bonins, and other Pacific Islands shall surrender to the Commander in Chief, U. S. Pacific Fleet.

(e) The Imperial Headquarters, its senior Commanders, and all ground, sea, air and auxiliary forces in the main islands of Japan, minor islands adjacent thereto, Korea South of 38 degrees North latitude, Ryukyus, and the Philippines shall surrender to the Commander in Chief, U. S. Army Forces, Pacific.

(f) The above indicated Commanders are the only representatives of the Allied Powers empowered to accept surrender, and all surrenders of Japanese Forces shall be made only to them or to their representatives. . . .

APPENDIX 6

UNITED STATES INITIAL POST-SURRENDER POLICY FOR JAPAN

PURPOSE OF THIS DOCUMENT

SEPTEMBER 6, 1945

This document is a statement of general initial policy relating to Japan after surrender. It has been approved by the President and distributed to the Supreme Commander for the Allied Powers and to appropriate United States departments and agencies for their guidance. It does not deal with all matters relating to the occupation of Japan requiring policy determinations. Such matters as are not included or are not fully covered herein have been or will be dealt with separately.

PART I—ULTIMATE OBJECTIVES

The ultimate objectives of the United States in regard to Japan, to which policies in the initial period must conform, are:

(a) To insure that Japan will not again become a menace to the United States or to the peace and security of the world.

167

(b) To bring about the eventual establishment of a peaceful and responsible government which will respect the rights of other states and will support the objectives of the United States as reflected in the ideals and principles of the Charter of the United Nations. The United States desires that this government should conform as closely as may be to principles of democratic self-government but it is not the responsibility of the Allied Powers to impose upon Japan any form of government not supported by the freely expressed will of the people.

These objectives will be achieved by the following principal means:

(a) Japan's sovereignty will be limited to the islands of Honshu, Hokkaido, Kyushu, Shikoku and such minor outlying islands as may be determined, in accordance with the Cairo Declaration and other agreements to which the United States is or may be a party.

(b) Japan will be completely disarmed and demilitarized. The authority of the militarists and the influence of militarism will be totally eliminated from her political, economic, and social life. Institutions expressive of the spirit of militarism and aggression will be vigorously suppressed.

(c) The Japanese people shall be encouraged to develop a desire for individual liberties and respect for fundamental human rights, particularly the freedoms of religion, assembly, speech, and the press. They shall also be encouraged to form democratic and representative organizations.

(d) The Japanese people shall be afforded opportunity to develop for themselves an economy which will permit the peacetime requirements of the population to be met.

PART II—ALLIED AUTHORITY

1. Military Occupation

There will be a military occupation of the Japanese home islands to carry into effect the surrender terms and further the achievement of the ultimate objectives stated above. The occupation shall have the character of an operation in behalf of the principal allied powers acting in the interests of the United Nations at war with Japan. For that reason, participation of the forces of other nations that have taken a leading part in the war against Japan will be welcomed and expected. The occupation forces will be under the command of a Supreme Commander designated by the United States.

Although evèry effort will be made, by consultation and by constitution of appropriate advisory bodies, to establish policies for the conduct of the occupation and the control of Japan which will satisfy the principal Allied powers, in the event of any differences of opinion among them, the policies of the United States will govern.

2. Relationship to Japanese Government

The authority of the Emperor and the Japanese Government will be subject to the Supreme Commander, who will possess all powers necessary to effectuate the surrender terms and to carry out the policies established for the conduct of the occupation and the control of Japan.

In view of the present character of Japanese society and the desire of the United States to attain its objectives with a minimum commitment of its forces and resources, the Supreme Commander will exercise his authority through Japanese governmental machinery and agencies, including the Emperor, to the extent that this satisfactorily furthers United States objectives. The Japanese Government will be permitted, under his instructions, to exercise the normal powers of government in matters of domestic administration. This policy, however, will be subject to the right and duty of the Supreme Commander to require changes in governmental machinery or personnel or to act directly if the Emperor or other Japanese authority does not satisfactorily meet the requirements of the Supreme Commander in effectuating the surrender terms. This policy, moreover, does not commit the Supreme Commander to support the Emperor or any other Japanese governmental authority in opposition to evolutionary changes looking toward the attainment of United States objectives. The policy is to use the existing form of Government in Japan, not to support it. Changes in the form of Government initiated by the Japanese people or government in the direction of modifying its feudal and authoritarian tendencies are to be permitted and favored. In the event that the effectuation of such changes involves the use of force by the Japanese people or government against persons opposed thereto, the Supreme Commander should intervene only where necessary to ensure the security of his forces and the attainment of all other objectives of the occupation.

3. Publicity as to Policies

The Japanese people, and the world at large, shall be kept fully informed of the objectives and policies of the occupation, and of progress made in their fulfilment.

PART III — POLITICAL

1. Disarmament and Demilitarization

Disarmament and demilitarization are the primary tasks of the military occupation and shall be carried out promptly and with determination. Every effort shall be made to bring home to the Japanese people the part played by the military and naval leaders, and those who collaborated with them, in bringing about the existing and future distress of the people.

Japan is not to have an army, navy, air force, secret police organization, or any civil aviation. Japan's ground, air and naval forces shall be disarmed and disbanded and the Japanese Imperial General Headquarters, the General Staff and all secret police organizations shall be dissolved. Military and naval matériel, military and naval vessels and military and naval installations, and military, naval and civilian aircraft shall be surrendered and shall be disposed of as required by the Supreme Commander.

High officials of the Japanese Imperial General Headquarters, and General Staff, other high military and naval officials of the Japanese Government, leaders of ultra-nationalist and militarist organizations and other important exponents of militarism and aggression will be taken into custody and held for future disposition. Persons who have been active exponents of militarism and militant nationalism will be removed and excluded from public office and from any other position of public or substantial private responsibility. Ultra-nationalistic or militaristic social, political, professional and commercial societies and institutions will be dissolved and prohibited.

Militarism and ultra-nationalism, in doctrine and practice, including para-military training, shall be eliminated from the educational system. Former career military and naval officers, both commissioned and non-commissioned, and all other exponents of militarism and ultra-nationalism shall be excluded from supervisory and teaching positions.

2. War Criminals

Persons charged by the Supreme Commander or appropriate United Nations Agencies with being war criminals, including those charged with having visited cruelties upon United Nations prisoners or other nationals, shall be arrested, tried and, if convicted, punished. Those wanted by another of the United Nations for offenses against its nationals, shall, if not wanted for trial or as witnesses or otherwise by the Supreme Commander, be turned over to the custody of such other nation.

3. Encouragement of Desire for Individual Liberties and Democratic Processes

Freedom of religious worship shall be proclaimed promptly on occupation. At the same time it should be made plain to the Japanese that ultra-nationalistic and militaristic organizations and movements will not be permitted to hide behind the cloak of religion.

The Japanese people shall be afforded opportunity and encouraged to become familiar with the history, institutions, culture, and the accomplishments of the United States and the other democracies. Association of personnel of the occupation forces with the Japanese population should be controlled, only to the extent necessary, to further the policies and objectives of the occupation.

Democratic political parties, with rights of assembly and public discussion, shall be encouraged, subject to the necessity for maintaining the security of the occupying forces.

Laws, decrees and regulations which establish discriminations on grounds of race, nationality, creed or political opinion shall be abrogated; those which conflict with the objectives and policies outlined in this document shall be repealed, suspended or amended as required; and agencies charged specifically with their enforcement shall be abolished or appropriately modified. Persons unjustly confined by Japanese authority on political grounds shall be released. The judicial, legal, and police systems shall be reformed as soon as practicable to conform to the policies set forth in Articles 1 and 3 of this Part III and thereafter shall be progressively influenced, to protect individual liberties and civil rights.

PART IV—ECONOMIC

1. Economic Demilitarization

The existing economic basis of Japanese military strength must be destroyed and not be permitted to revive.

Therefore, a program will be enforced containing the following elements, among others; the immediate cessation and future prohibition of production of all goods designed for the equipment, maintenance, or use of any military force or establishment; the imposition of a ban upon any specialized facilities for the production or repair of implements of war, including naval vessels and all forms of aircraft; the institution of a system of inspection and control over selected elements in Japanese economic activity to prevent concealed or disguised military preparation; the elimination in Japan of those selected industries or branches of production whose chief value to Japan is in preparing for war; the prohibition of specialized research and instruction directed to the development of war-making power; and the limitation of the size and character of Japan's heavy industries to its future peaceful requirements, and restriction of Japanese merchant shipping to the extent required to accomplish the objectives of demilitarization.

The eventual disposition of those existing production facilities within Japan which are to be eliminated in accord with this program, as between conversion to other uses, transfer abroad, and scrapping will be determined after inventory. Pending decision, facilities readily convertible for civilian production should not be destroyed, except in emergency situations.

2. Promotion of Democratic Forces

Encouragement shall be given and favor shown to the development of organizations in labor, industry, and agriculture, organized on a democratic basis. Policies shall be favored which permit a wide distribution of income and of the ownership of the means of production and trade.

Those forms of economic activity, organization and leadership shall be favored that are deemed likely to strengthen the peaceful disposition of the Japanese people, and to make it difficult to command or direct economic activity in support of military ends.

To this end it shall be the policy of the Supreme Commander:

(a) To prohibit the retention in or selection for places of importance in the economic field of individuals who do not direct future Japanese economic effort solely towards peaceful ends; and

(b) To favor a program for the dissolution of the large industrial and banking combinations which have exercised control of a great part of Japan's trade and industry.

3. Resumption of Peaceful Economic Activity

The policies of Japan have brought down upon the people great economic destruction and confronted them with the prospect of economic difficulty and suffering. The plight of Japan is the direct outcome of its own behavior, and the Allies will not undertake the burden of repairing the damage. It can be repaired only if the Japanese people renounce all military aims and apply themselves diligently and with single purpose to the ways of peaceful living. It will be necessary for them to undertake physical reconstruction, deeply to reform the nature and direction of their economic activities and institutions, and to find useful employment for their people along lines adapted to and devoted to peace. The Allies have no intention of imposing conditions which would prevent the accomplishment of these tasks in due time.

Japan will be expected to provide goods and services to meet the needs of the occupying forces to the extent that this can be effected without causing starvation, widespread disease and acute physical distress.

The Japanese authorities will be expected, and if necessary directed, to maintain, develop and enforce programs that serve the following purposes:

(a) To avoid acute economic distress.

(b) To assure just and impartial distribution of available supplies.

(c) To meet the requirements for reparations deliveries agreed upon by the Allied Governments.

(d) To facilitate the restoration of Japanese economy so that the reasonable peaceful requirements of the population can be satisfied.

In this connection, the Japanese authorities on their own responsibility shall be permitted to establish and administer controls over economic activities, including essential national public services, finance, banking, and production and distribution of essential commodities, subject to the approval and review of the Supreme Commander in order to assure their conformity with the objectives of the occupation.

4. Reparations and Restitution

Reparations. Reparations for Japanese aggression shall be made:

(a) Through the transfer—as may be determined by the appropriate Allied authorities—of Japanese property located outside of the territories to be retained by Japan.

(b) Through the transfer of such goods or existing capital equipment and facilities as are not necessary for a peaceful Japanese economy or the supplying of the occupying forces. Exports other than those directed to be shipped on reparation account or as restitution may be made only to those recipients who agree to provide necessary imports in exchange or agree to pay for such exports in foreign exchange. No form of reparation shall be exacted which will interfere with or prejudice the program for Japan's demilitarization.

Restitution. Full and prompt restitution will be required of all identifiable looted property.

5. Fiscal, Monetary, and Banking Policies

The Japanese authorities will remain responsible for the management and direction of the domestic fiscal, monetary, and credit policies subject to the approval and review of the Supreme Commander.

6. International Trade and Financial Relations

Japan shall be permitted eventually to resume normal trade relations with the rest of the world. During occupation and under suitable controls, Japan will be permitted to purchase from foreign countries raw materials and other goods that it may need for peaceful purposes, and to export goods to pay for approved imports.

Control is to be maintained over all imports and exports of goods and foreign exchange and financial transactions. Both the policies followed in the exercise of these controls and their actual administration shall be subject to the approval and supervision of the Supreme Commander in order to make sure that they are not contrary to the policies of the occupying authorities, and in particular that all foreign purchasing power that Japan may acquire is utilized only for essential needs.

7. Japanese Property Located Abroad

Existing Japanese external assets and existing Japanese assets located in territories detached from Japan under the terms of surrender, including assets owned in whole or part by the Imperial Household and Government, shall be revealed to the occupying authorities and held for disposition according to the decision of the Allied authorities.

8. Equality of Opportunity for Foreign Enterprise within Japan

The Japanese authorities shall not give, or permit any Japanese business organization to give, exclusive or preferential opportunity or terms to the enterprise of any foreign country, or cede to such enterprise control of any important branch of economic activity.

9. Imperial Household Property

Imperial Household property shall not be exempted from any action necessary to carry out the objectives of the occupation.

APPENDIX 7

AGREEMENT OF FOREIGN MINISTERS AT MOSCOW ON ESTABLISHING FAR EASTERN COMMISSION AND ALLIED COUNCIL FOR JAPAN

DECEMBER 27, 1945

The Foreign Ministers of the Union of Soviet Socialist Republics, the United Kingdom, and the United States of America met in Moscow from December 16 to December 26, 1945, in accordance with the decision of the Crimea Conference, confirmed at the Berlin Conference, that there should be periodic consultation between them. At the meeting of the three Foreign Ministers, discussion took place on an informal and exploratory basis and agreement was reached on:

FAR EASTERN COMMISSION AND ALLIED COUNCIL FOR JAPAN

A. Far Eastern Commission

Agreement was reached, with the concurrence of China, for the establishment of a Far Eastern Commission to take the place of the Far Eastern Advisory Commission. The Terms of Reference for the Far Eastern Commission are as follows:

I. Establishment of the Commission A Far Eastern Commission is hereby established composed of the representatives of the Union of Soviet Socialist Republics, United Kingdom, United States, China, France, The Netherlands, Canada, Australia, New Zealand, India, and the Philippine Commonwealth.

II. Functions A. The functions of the Far Eastern Commission shall be:

1. To formulate the policies, principles, and standards in conformity with which the fulfillment by Japan of its obligations under the Terms of Surrender may be accomplished.

2. To review, on the request of any member, any directive issued by the Supreme Commander for the Allied Powers or any action taken by the Supreme Commander involving policy decisions within the jurisdiction of the Commission.

3. To consider such other matters as may be assigned to it by agreement among the participating Governments reached in accordance with the voting procedure provided for in Article V-2 hereunder.

B. The Commission shall not make recommendations with regard to the conduct of military operations nor with regard to territorial adjustments.

C. The Commission in its activities will proceed from the fact that there has been formed an Allied Council for Japan and will respect existing control machinery in Japan, including the chain of command from the United States Government to the Supreme Commander and the Supreme Commander's command of occupation forces.

III. Functions of the United States Government 1. The United States Government shall prepare directives in accordance with the policy decisions of the Commission and shall transmit them to the Supreme Commander through the appropriate United States Government agency. The Supreme Commander shall be charged with the implementation of the directives which express the policy decisions of the Commission.

2. If the Commission decides that any directive or action reviewed in accordance with Article II-A-2 should be modified, its decision shall be regarded as a policy decision.

3. The United States Government may issue interim directives to the Supreme Commander pending action by the Commission whenever urgent matters arise not covered by policies already formulated by the Commission; provided that any directives dealing with fundamental changes in the Japanese constitutional structure or in the regime of control, or dealing with a change in the Japanese Government as a whole will be issued only following consultation and following the attainment of agreement in the Far Eastern Commission.

4. All directives issued shall be filed with the Commission.

IV. Other Methods of Consultation The establishment of the Commission shall not preclude the use of other methods of consultation on Far Eastern issues by the participating Governments.

V. Composition 1. The Far Eastern Commission shall consist of one representative of each of the States party to this agreement. The membership of the Commission may be increased by agreement among the participating Powers as conditions warrant by the addition of representatives of other United Nations in the Far East or having territories therein. The Commission shall provide for full and adequate consultations, as occasion may require, with representatives of the United Nations not members of the Commission in regard to matters before the Commission which are of particular concern to such nations.

2. The Commission may take action by less than unanimous vote provided that action shall have the concurrence of as least a majority of all the representatives including the representatives of the four following Powers: United States, United Kingdom, Union of Soviet Socialist Republics and China.

VI. Location and Organization 1. The Far Eastern Commission shall have its headquarters in Washington. It may meet at other places as occasion requires, including Tokyo, if and when it deems it desirable to do so. It may make such arrangements through the Chairman as may be practicable for consultation with the Supreme Commander for the Allied Powers.

2. Each representative on the Commission may be accompanied by an appropriate staff comprising both civilian and military representation.

3. The Commission shall organize its secretariat, appoint such committees as may be deemed advisable, and otherwise perfect its organization and procedure.

VII. Termination The Far Eastern Commission shall cease to function when a decision to that effect is taken by the concurrence of at least a majority of all the representatives including the representatives of the four following Powers: United States, United Kingdom, Union of Soviet Socialist Republics and China. Prior to the termination of its functions the Commission shall transfer to any interim or permanent security organization of which the participating governments are members those functions which may appropriately be transferred.

It was agreed that the Government of the United States on behalf of the four Powers should present the Terms of Reference to the other Governments specified in Article I and invite them to participate in the Commission on the revised basis.

B. Allied Council for Japan

The following agreement was also reached, with the concurrence of China, for the establishment of an Allied Council for Japan:

1. There shall be established an Allied Council with its seat in Tokyo under the chairmanship of the Supreme Commander for the Allied Powers (or his Deputy) for the purpose of consulting with and advising the Supreme Commander in regard to the implementation of the Terms of Surrender, the occupation and control of Japan, and of directives supplementary thereto; and for the purpose of exercising the control authority herein granted.

2. The membership of the Allied Council shall consist of the Supreme Commander (or his Deputy) who shall be Chairman and United States member; a Union of Soviet Socialist Republics member; a Chinese member; and a member representing jointly the

United Kingdom, Australia, New Zealand, and India.

3. Each member shall be entitled to have an appropriate staff consisting of military and civilian advisers.

4. The Allied Council shall meet not less often than once every two weeks.

5. The Supreme Commander shall issue all orders for the implementation of the Terms of Surrender, the occupation and control of Japan, and directives supplementary thereto. In all cases action will be carried out under and through the Supreme Commander who is the sole executive authority for the Allied Powers in Japan. He will consult and advise with the Council in advance of the issuance of orders on matters of substance, the exigencies of the situation permitting. His decisions upon these matters shall be controlling.

6. If, regarding the implementation of policy decisions of the Far Eastern Commission on questions concerning a change in the regime of control, fundamental changes in the Japanese constitutional structure, and a change in the Japanese Government as a whole, a member of the Council disagrees with the Supreme Commander (or his Deputy), the Supreme Commander will withhold the issuance of orders on these questions pending agreement thereon in the Far Eastern Commission.

7. In cases of necessity the Supreme Commander may take decisions concerning the change of individual Ministers of the Japanese Government, or concerning the filling of vacancies created by the resignation of individual cabinet members, after appropriate preliminary consultation with the representatives of the other Allied Powers on the Allied Council.

Index

Acheson, Dean, 29–30, 54, 125, 148
Allen, George, 121
Allied Council for Japan (*known in planning as* Allied Control Council *or* Allied Military Council)
  Byrnes's attitude to, 52–53, 56–58, 67, 75–76
  favored by British, 45
  MacArthur and, 58, 60, 68, 110, 129–31
  in Moscow Conference (1945), 89–91, 107, 109–10, 114, 116
  text of agreement, 179–80
  proposed name changed, 74, 90–91
  Russian participation in, 129–32
  Russian proposals for, 28, 37, 42, 46–47, 50, 71–76
  in Stalin-Harriman talks, 60–65
Atcheson, George, Jr., 130, 138
Atomic bomb, 6–9, 14, 15
Atomic energy, discussed at Moscow Conference (1945), 87, 113, 120, 123, 125
"Atomic" toast of Stalin, 107–8
Attlee, Clement, 18, 41
Australia, 91

Far Eastern (Advisory) Commission and, 28, 133–34, 142
Austria, provisional government in, 101–2, 103

"Baltic republics," 100
Belgium, 100
Beria, Lavrenti, 59
Bevin, Ernest, 53–54
  Byrnes and, 31–32, 113
  in London Conference (1945), 31–32, 38, 39, 48
  Molotov and, 31, 39
  Moscow Conference (1945) and, 79–80, 83, 86–91, 97, 99, 104, 106, 112–13
  on Russian and U.S. aspirations, 89–90
Bidault, Georges
  in London Conference (1945), 32, 34, 37, 38
  personality of, 32
Blakeslee, George H., 135n, 139n, 141n
Bulgaria, 124
  Allied Control Council in, 64
  Communist-oriented government in, 104–6, 121–23

Ethridge report on, 102–5
peace treaty with, 33–36, 42, 44–45, 98–101, 106
Byrnes, James F., 14, 27
  Allied Council for Japan and, 52–53, 56–58, 67, 72, 75–76
  Bevin and, 31–32, 113
  Chicago *Tribune* comment on, 85
  Far Eastern (Advisory) Commission and, 28, 45–46, 51–53, 68–69
  in London Conference (1945), 30–39, 42, 44–50
  Molotov and, 31, 112
  Moscow Conference (1945) and, 78–100, 104–6, 108–14
  conference proposed by Byrnes, 78–80
  his arrival in Moscow, 85
  his broadcast afterwards, 114
  meetings with Stalin, 95, 100–1, 105, 107–8
  policy of sparse reporting to Washington, 124–26
  Truman's reaction, 119–26

Cairo Declaration, 10–11, 19
  text of, 155–56
Chiang Kai-shek, 10, 11, 18, 81
  neutral policy of, 32
  Russians and, 20, 94
Chicago *Tribune*, 85
China
  American prewar attitude toward, 4, 5
  American troops in, 19, 81–83, 87–89, 93–96
  effect of sudden end of war on, 9
  evacuation of Japanese from, 81–83, 93–95
  Far Eastern (Advisory) Commission and, 56, 133, 136
  in London Conference (1945), 32, 34, 37–38, 47–48
  Russia and
    agreement with Nationalist China, 20–21, 95

Harriman's advice, 54
relations with Communists, 20–21, 27, 94, 144, 150
Russian troops in Manchuria, 8–9, 28, 81–83, 88–89, 94–95
Stalin's policy, 55–56
Chinese Communists
  Japanese peace treaty and, 146, 148, 149
  in North China after war, 81–82, 94–95
  possibility of Nationalist accord with, 82n
  Russia and, 20–21, 27, 94, 144, 150
  Stalin on, 95
Churchill, Winston, 6, 10
Clark-Kerr, Sir Archibald, 105
Clifford, Clark, 121
Connelly, Matthew, 121
Control councils
  in Germany, 72
  for Japan, *see* Allied Council for Japan
  in Southeastern Europe, 56, 60–62, 64, 70, 71, 76
Council of Foreign Ministers, *see* London Conference; Moscow Conference

Daniels, Jonathan, 121n, 122n
Dardanelles (Black Sea) Straits, 34, 35, 112, 122, 123
Darien, 20, 94
Davies, John Paton, 27
De Gaulle, Charles, 34
Derevyanko, Gen. Kuzma, 63, 64–65, 127–29
  in Allied Council for Japan, 129–32
Donnelly, Desmond, 38n
Dulles, John Foster, 49, 148, 149n
Dunn, James C., 51

Eden, Sir Anthony, 48
Ehrenburg, Ilya, 105
Emperor of Japan
  Russian attitude toward, 13, 16, 127

in surrender negotiations, 14, 15, 162–63
Ethridge report, 102–5, 113
Evatt, Herbert V., 134

Far Eastern Commission (*known in planning as* Far Eastern Advisory Commission)
British attitude to, 28, 45
Byrnes and, 28, 45–46, 51–53, 68–69
creation of, 26–28
first meeting called, 51, 56
first meetings of, 68–69, 76–77
Japanese peace treaty and, 145, 147
members of, $26n$
Moscow Conference (1945) discussions of, 89–92, 107, 108–9, 114, 116, 138
text of agreement, 176–79
new constitution for Japan discussed in, 137, 138, 140
1946 elections discussed in, 135–37
proposed name changed, 90
proposed voting procedure in, 69, 70
Russian attitude to, 45–47, 55, 57–58, 60, 65, 70
Russian participation in, 132–35, 140–44
Finland
elections in, 104
peace treaty with, 33, 98–99, 101
Formosa, return to China of, 11, 148
4-3-2 formula, 98–99
France
in Far Eastern Commission, 133, 136
in London Conference (1945), 32, 34, 37, 38

General Order No. 1, 12, 18–19, 93
text of, 164–66
Germany
Allied Control Council in, 72

central administration for, 34
reparations from, 34
Graham, Gen. Wallace, 121
Great Britain, *see* United Kingdom
Greece, 34, 35, 99, 103
British forces in, 83, 87–89, 104, 112
Gromyko, Andrei, 133, 150

Halifax, Lord, 133
Harriman, W. Averell
Allied Control Council and, 60–65, 69–76
Far Eastern (Advisory) Commission and, 26–28
Japanese surrender and, 16–17
London Conference (1945) and, 44–45
meeting with MacArthur, 128–29
meeting with Stalin (Oct., 1945), 51–54, 57–66
Moscow Conference (1945) and, 83, 86–87, 91, 93, 105, 124
Harsch, Joseph, 117–18
Higashi-Kuni, Prince, 138
Hiroshima, 8, 15
Hodges, Gen. Courtney H., 96, $97n$
Hokkaido, Russian request to occupy, 20, $64n$
Holland, 100
Hopkins, Harry, in May, 1945, conversation with Stalin, 13–14
Hungary
Allied Control Council in, 60–61, 70, 71
peace treaty with, 33, 45, 98–101
provisional government of, 101–5

India, 91, 100, 108
Indonesia, 88
Initial Post-Surrender Policy for Japan, 12, 23–25, 30, 36
text of, 167–75
Iran, 34
Soviet troops in, 78, 89, 112, 122, 123
Italy, peace treaty with, 33, 35, 37, 38, 98, 101

Japan
changes in American prewar attitude toward, 3–5
demilitarization of, 24, 127–28
dropping of atomic bomb on, 6–9
effect of cold war on, 143–44, 146
elections in (1946), 135–37
London Conference (1945) and, 35–37, 42, 44–47
Moscow Conference (1945) and, 101, 104, 107–10, 114, 123
new constitution for, 137–42
1966 Russian agreement with, 150
occupation of
basic U.S. policy, 25
General Order No. 1, 12, 18–19, 93, 164–66
initial memorandum to MacArthur (Aug., 1945), 22–23
Initial Post-Surrender Policy, 12, 23–25, 30, 36, 167–75
MacArthur appointed Supreme Commander, 16–17, 43
proposed Allied participation in occupation army, 57–58, 60–61, 69, 75
Russian policy, see Russia—policy on occupation of Japan
U.S. desire for unified command, 7–8
U.S. policy as supreme, 25, 57
see also Allied Council for Japan; Far Eastern Commission; MacArthur; Potsdam Declaration and Agreement
peace treaty with, 144–50
surrender of, 12, 17
orders to military commanders, 17–19, 164–66
Russian attitude, 13, 19–20
see also Potsdam Declaration and Agreement
territorial renunciations of, 11, 24, 147
Truman's policy on, 122
Johnson, Louis, 146
Johnson, Nelson T., 77

Joint Chiefs of Staff, 94, 97n, 146
Jowitt, Lord, 79

Karafuto, see Sakhalin, south
Kennan, George F., 27, 51–52
Kiel Canal, 122–23
King, Mackenzie, 113
Kislenko, Gen., 131–32
Korea, 9
Moscow Conference (1945) discussions on, 96–98
North, 28, 144–45
origin of 38th parallel in, 19
Truman's policy on, 122, 123
Korean war, 131, 146–47
possible reasons for outbreak of, 144–45
Krock, Arthur, 117
Kurile Islands
in Japanese peace treaty, 148
Japanese surrender in, 19–20
promised to Russia, 11

Leahy, Adm. William D., 39–40, 121
Locke, Edwin A., Jr., 58n
London Conference (1945), 30–50
adjournment of, 47–48
aims of each government at, 33–34
Japanese question and, 35–37, 42, 44–47
long meetings of, 33
participation of all members in, 35, 37–41, 47
representatives at, 31–32

MacArthur, Gen. Douglas, 12
Allied Council for Japan and, 58, 60, 68, 110, 129–31
appointed Supreme Commander, 16–17, 43
bold exercise of authority by, 28–30
Far Eastern Commission and, 134–37
independent attitude of, 58n
Moscow Conference (1945) and, 114–15

new Japanese constitution and,
137–42
1946 elections and, 135–37
objects to Initial Post-Surrender
Policy, 23
peace treaty with Japan and, 147
policy in Japan of, 77
Russians and, 63–65, 128–38
on Stalin's policy, 129
McCloy, John J., 23
McCoy, Gen. Frank R., 77, 133, 134
Malinovsky, Marshal Rodion, 9n
Manchuria, 5, 6, 11
Japanese surrender in, 19
Russian special rights in, 11, 20
Russian troops in, 8–9, 28, 81–83,
88–89, 94–95, 107
Mao Tse-tung, 95
Marshall, Gen. George C., 18, 23
in China, 82–83, 93–96, 125
Molotov, V. M., 8, 75
Allied Control Council and, 37,
42, 46–47, 50, 70–73
Bevin and, 31, 39
Byrnes and, 31, 112
Far Eastern (Advisory) Commission and, 52–53, 56
Japanese surrender and, 12, 14,
16–17
in London Conference (1945),
30–33, 35–39, 44, 46–47, 50
Moscow Conference (1945) and,
79, 83, 86–89, 91, 93–100, 104–
6, 108
Mountbatten, Adm. Lord Louis,
88
Moscow Conference (1945), 78–126
agenda for, 81–84
agreements on Japan at, 107–10
text of, 176–80
atomic energy at, 87, 113, 120,
123, 125
crucial importance of, 80
editorial reactions to, 115–18
peace treaties discussed at, 78–79,
98–106, 123
Truman's reaction to, 118–26
unrelenting schedule of, 86

Nagasaki, 8, 15
New Zealand, in Far Eastern Com-
mission, 133, 134
Nimitz, Adm. Chester W., 19
Norway, 100
Novikov, N. V., 133, 134, 136–37

Outer Mongolia, in Yalta agreements, 11

Page, Edward, 64n (see Locke)
Parrott, Lindesay, 115n
Peace treaties
in Harriman-Stalin meeting
(Oct., 1945), 59, 62
in London Conference (1945),
33–45
in Moscow Conference (1945),
78–79, 98–106, 123
Pearl Harbor attack, 5
Pescadores, the, 11, 148
Phillips, Cabell, 124
Poland, 102, 104, 124
Port Arthur, 20
Potsdam Conference, 7, 31, 123–24
Potsdam Declaration and Agreement, 11–12
occupation of Japan and, 13, 137,
138, 141
participation in Council of Foreign Ministers and, 37–41
peace treaty with Japan and, 145,
147, 149
Russian attitude to, 14–15
text of American reply to Japanese qualified acceptance,
162–163
text of Declaration, 160–61

Rhine-Danube waterway, 122, 123
Roberts, Gen. F. N., 74
Roosevelt, Franklin D., 6, 10, 11
Rosenmann, Samuel, 121
Ross, Charles, 119–21
Rumania, 124
Allied Control Council in, 56, 60–
61, 64
Communist-oriented government
in, 102–6, 121–23

peace treaty with, 33–36, 39, 42, 44–45, 98–101, 106
Russia
  China and
    agreement with Nationalist Government, 20–21, 95
    Harriman's advice, 54
    relations with Communists, 20–21, 27, 94, 144, 150
    Russian troops in Manchuria, 81–83, 88–89, 94–95
  entry into war against Japan
    goal of American policy, 5–7
    invasion of Manchuria, 8–9, 107
    Russian promise to enter war, 5–6, 11, 13
    territories promised to Russia, 11
  Japanese peace treaty and, 145–50
  1966 agreement between Japan and, 150
  policy on occupation of Japan
    agreement on Supreme Commander, 16–17, 43
    dislike of U.S. policy, 24–25
    relationship to Southeastern Europe, 42, 44–45, 101, 104, 117–18
    Russian complaint that they are not informed, 63, 72
    Shidehara cabinet opposed, 67–68
    Stalin's May, 1945, statement, 13–14
    see also Allied Council for Japan; Far Eastern Commission
  Stalin's policy, 55–56
Russo-Japanese War, 3–4

Sakhalin, south (Karafuto)
  in Japanese peace treaty, 148
  Japanese surrender in, 19
  promised to Russia, 11
Sebald, William J., 130
Shidehara, Baron, 67–68, 138
Soong, T. V., 8, 56

Soviet Union, see Russia
Stalin, Joseph, 48
  "atomic" toast of, 107–8
  on Chinese Communists, 95
  invasion of Manchuria and, 8, 107
  London Conference (1945) and, 41, 42
  MacArthur on policy of, 129
  meetings with Harriman
    Harriman's farewell call, 127–28
    Oct. 1945 meeting, 51–54, 57–66
  Moscow Conference (1945) and, 95, 98, 100–1, 105, 107–8, 112–13
  occupation of Japan and, 13–14, 17, 19
    Advisory Commission and Control Council, 57–66, 69, 73
    opposes Russian troops in Japan, 61, 69
  Potsdam Declaration and, 12, 15
Stevens, Edmund, 116n

Tientsin, 95
Truman, Harry S, 112, 113
  and Byrnes' decisions at Moscow, 119–126
  Japanese surrender and, 12, 14, 20
  London Conference (1945) and, 33, 39–42
  messages to Stalin from, 39–41
  Moscow Conference (1945) and, 118–26
  occupation of Japan and, 7–8, 22, 23n, 29
    Russian participation in occupation, 42–43, 76
  on peace treaty with Japan, 147
Turkey, Russia and, 78, 89, 112

Ukraine, 100
"Unconditional surrender" of Japan, 11

United Kingdom (Great Britain)
Far Eastern (Advisory) Commission and, 28, 45, 133–34
in occupation of Japan, 75
See also Bevin
United Nations General Assembly, 78

Vandenberg, Arthur H., 120
Vasilevski, Marshal Alexander, 17
Vaughan, Gen. Harry H., 121
Vietnam, 150
Vishinsky, Andrei, 102, 105

Wang Shih-chieh, in London Conference (1945), 32, 37–38, 47–48
Washington Naval Treaties, 4
Wedemeyer, Gen. Albert, 81*n*
Wei Tao-ming, 133
Wherry, Kenneth S., 30
White Russia, 100

Yalta agreements, 6, 11, 78, 102
text of agreement regarding Japan, 157–58
Yoshida, Shigeru, 146
Yugoslavia, 99

HERBERT FEIS, economist and Pulitzer Prize winner in History, has had a distinguished career as a scholar, a writer, and as an influental adviser to the U. S. government. He was graduated from Harvard in 1916 and took his Ph. D. there in 1921. He taught at Harvard, at the University of Kansas, and from 1926 to 1929 he was head of the Economics Department at the University of Cincinnati. From 1930 to 1931 he was on the staff of the Council of Foreign Relations. In 1931 he began a period of government service, as Adviser on International Economic Affairs to the Department of State (1931-1943), chief technical adviser for the American delegation at the World Economic and Monetary Conference in London (1933), special adviser at the Conference of American Republics (1936, 1938, 1939), Special Consultant to the Secretary of War (1944-47), and member of the State Department's policy planning staff (1950-51). He has been a member of the Institute for Advanced Study and a Guggenheim fellow.

Mr. Feis has written many books, including: *Europe: The World's Banker 1870-1914* (1930); *Seen from E.A.: Three International Episodes* (1946); *The Spanish Story* (1948); *The Road to Pearl Harbor* (1950); *The Diplomacy of the Dollar* (1950); *The China Tangle* (1953); *Churchill-Roosevelt-Stalin* (1957); *Between War and Peace: The Potsdam Conference* (1960); *Japan Subdued* (1961); *Foreign Aid and Foreign Policy* (1964); and *Contest Over Japan* (1967).